PENGUIN BOOKS
Under Cover

Thomas L. Bonn is Media Librarian at the State University of New York College at Cortland. Recipient of several grants for the study of paperback publishing history, he frequently writes on topics connected with paperbacks and their cover art and is contributing editor of *Paperback Quarterly: Journal of Mass-Market Paperback History.* He resides with his wife, Ellen, and two children in Etna, New York.

John Tebbel is the author of the four-volume *History of Book Publishing in the United States,* for which he has twice been nominated for a Pulitzer Prize. He is the former chairman of the Journalism Department at New York University, where he started the first graduate-level program in book publishing in this country.

UnderCover

AN ILLUSTRATED HISTORY OF AMERICAN MASS MARKET PAPERBACKS

by Thomas L. Bonn

Foreword by John Tebbel

PENGUIN BOOKS

For Murph and the millions like her
who have waited "until it
comes out in paperback"

Penguin Books Ltd, Harmondsworth,
Middlesex, England
Penguin Books, 625 Madison Avenue,
New York, New York 10022, U.S.A.
Penguin Books Australia Ltd, Ringwood,
Victoria, Australia
Penguin Books Canada Limited, 2801 John Street,
Markham, Ontario, Canada L3R 1B4
Penguin Books (N.Z.) Ltd, 182-190 Wairau Road,
Auckland 10, New Zealand

First published 1982

Copyright © Thomas L. Bonn, 1982
Foreword copyright © John Tebbel, 1982
All rights reserved

LIBRARY OF CONGRESS CATALOGING IN PUBLICATION DATA
Bonn, Thomas L.
Under cover.
Includes index.
1. Paperbacks—Publishing—United States—History.
2. Publishers and publishing—United States—History.
3. Book industries and trade—United States—History.
I. Title.
Z479.B63   070.5′0973   81-21035
ISBN 0 14 00.6071 5   AACR2

Printed in the United States of America by
Halliday Lithograph Corporation,
West Hanover, Massachusetts
Set in Century Schoolbook
Designed by Beth Tondreau

The author wishes to thank the following for permission
to reproduce covers in this book: Ace Books; Avon Books;
Ballantine Books; Bantam Books, Inc.; Harry Bennett;
James Campbell; Dell Publishing Co., Inc.; Fawcett
Books; H. Thomas Hall; Jove Publications, Inc.; Robert
E. McGinnis; The New American Library, Inc.; Pocket
Books, a Simon & Schuster Division of Gulf & Western
Corporation; Popular Library; and Warner Books, Inc.

Contents

PART II · COVER ART AND DESIGN

A NOTE ON THE BOOK DIMENSIONS
Since 1939 American mass market paperbacks have been classified by one of two dimensions, small and large. The small size, pioneered by Pocket Books, measured approximately 4¼″ x 6⅜″. This size, at a disadvantage when mixed with the larger format on display racks, disappeared for the most part in the early sixties. The longer dimension, roughly 4¼″ x 7″, is the standard for the industry today. Readers should be aware that the relative proportions of the reproductions of covers in this book do not necessarily indicate those of the actual books themselves.

Contents

Foreword

"Paperback revolution" has become a cliché both in and out of the book business without any clear understanding on the part of most people who use it that this "revolution" has been going on for nearly two centuries now. It must be the longest such event in world history.

The events of our own time so often cited are no more revolutionary than the craze for cheap softcover editions that swept the country in the two decades before the Civil War, creating such a mass market of addicts that bales of paperbacks had to be shipped to the various camps of the Union Army during the war. (The Confederacy was less well served, since its short supply of paper and ink left the South barely able to maintain any kind of publishing.)

Sadly enough, wars have always been prime movers in this continuing revolution. Apparently the boredom of camp life will drive men to read books who never much bothered with them before. For millions, the result was a personal voyage of discovery, creating peacetime armies of readers who often passed the habit on to their children.

These freshly minted audiences must have been struck most of all by the wide variety of the world of books. Those who wanted entertainment simply to pass the time found it in abundance, and in dozens of forms. Those who wanted to learn, whether in the disinterested quest for more knowledge about the world or for information that would help them play a better part in it, discovered a resource richer than any gold mine.

After the Second World War, when the millions of paperbacks distributed by the Armed Services Editions had created a new mass market never realized in the past, the explosion of paperbacks (which those unfamiliar with publishing history believed was brand new) resulted in a steady and often spectacular growth of the softcover business, until it has now come to dominate trade publishing and to be an increasingly valuable adjunct to nearly every other branch of the industry.

Paperbacks have added immeasurably to the information and entertainment available to people everywhere in the world. Their easy portability has taken books out of the living room and bedroom into airplanes, trains, buses, and automobiles. Once scorned by libraries, paperbacks now commonly have their own niche there. They are traded as commodities, passed along from person to person until they fall apart, read in every conceivable kind of location.

Historians of culture and of the history of ideas have only begun to scratch the surface of what these books have meant to American life, much less to the cultures of other countries. For some critics, true, they have not been an unmixed blessing. The several categories of romance novels, which register the highest sales figures of any genre, are regularly deplored for their lack of any quality other than entertainment. They were deplored in much the same terms before the Civil War, and in even stronger words before the end of the century. We also hear talk from time to time about the sexual content of paperback novels, on and between the covers. Yet softcover nonfiction books about sex have made sound information available to millions in a country where sexual ignorance has made therapy in this field a thriving specialty.

Today the immense variety that once characterized the range of hardcover publishing is also available in soft covers, and at prices that have made it possible in an inflationary era for people who might otherwise not have been able to do so to keep on buying and reading books. Indeed, paperbacks have become so important a part of contemporary life, at least among those who are literate, that it is almost impossible to imagine life without them.

Tom Bonn has done a service to book people as well as to

readers in writing *Under Cover*. With a scholar's skill and a historian's viewpoint, he has brought together the many tangled threads that make up the fabric of this publishing colossus and shown us the whole phenomenon, intact. Moreover, he has provided the perspective so many of us have lacked by tracing its historical origins and development.

As a historian of publishing, I not only applaud what he has done but hope that it will inspire other scholars to examine this industry's history in more detail. Further studies could well add insights to our understanding of America that have not been available before. The paperback book has been an important part of our culture for more than a hundred years, and never more so than now. It richly deserves further attention. *Under Cover* is a splendid beginning.

—John Tebbel

Acknowledgments

In writing a short history of any major American industry one must describe major trends and events while ignoring hundreds of important occurrences, which to some may appear more significant than much of the information presented. The events covered here, in my opinion, best illustrate how mass market paperback publishing became established in the United States. To those authors, illustrators, and publishers of the American mass market paperback industry who may feel differently I plead for understanding.

To understand American paperback publishing it is necessary to be introduced to the four main functions of a paperback publisher: editorial, production, marketing, and design. The first three of these functions are very lightly drawn here. Aside from the content of a book—the basis for the entire industry—nothing draws the attention of the paperback author, publisher, bookseller, and the public more than the design and artwork on paperback books. Hence my emphasis throughout on design considerations.

It is not possible to recognize all of the hundreds of people who aided my research over the past ten years: book publishers, designers, and art directors, and especially cover artists, who have given so generously of their time and answered my many queries.

I also regret not being able to identify the creators of every illustration shown. The absence of clear signatures on the covers often makes positive identification impossible. Nor has it always been possible to clear permission to use the cover designs shown in this text. Few publishers have retained records that reach back into the early days of paperback publishing recording ownership. Nor do they have the current addresses of artists who worked in those early years.

Special thanks must go to John Tebbel and Marilyn Abel. For over a decade both have repeatedly encouraged and aided this project. Thanks also to Brother Conan Moran, Carol Nemeyer, Harold Laskey, and Felix Reichmann, mentors and teachers, each of whom in different ways inspired this text. Recognition must also be given to the Friends of the Tompkins County Public Library, whose industry and dedication annually produce a library book sale, from which many of the cover designs were obtained.

During the course of the writing, newfound friends—writers, collectors, and vintage-paperback booksellers—have given me valued and continuous aid in my search for specific illustrations and artist identification: William Lyles, Geoffrey O'Brien, Bill Crider, Peter Manesis, Michael Barson, Lance Casebeer, Billy C. Lee, and, in particular, M. C. "Bunker" Hill and Stan Hicks.

This book could not have been written had I not received financial support from the Research Foundation of the State University of New York and moral support and encouragement from the staff and students at Cortland State College, especially Selby Gration, Carl Burr, and Elaine Dunbar.

To members of my family, both real and adopted—Ellen, Fred, Amy, and Piet—the joys of this volume reflect your love, patience, and understanding.

Preface

It happened in the mid-1950s during my first week as a college freshman. Shouldering my way into the campus bookstore with hundreds of equally lost classmates, I discovered a half dozen wire racks stocked with *paperbacks*. Dirty books!

In the middle-class neighborhood where I grew up, "pocket books" were found in Golden's Drugstore, across the street from our church and school. They were displayed on revolving wire racks, between the greeting cards and magazines. Entering Golden's for a frozen Milky Way candy bar, I would cast amazed glances at the fleshy female victims of the mayhem and murder exploding on the glossy covers. Bare backs, thighs, and breasts barely restrained by flimsy blouses or slipping nightgowns tumbled off the foreground of the covers. A half-hidden man usually leered in the background. Obviously he had just done or was about to do something awful to the blond innocent. Sometimes the cover furnished a keyhole or window to peek through. Most often, however, illustrations bled the full width of the front cover. There were also books of corny cartoons; even they were sexy, with fantastically proportioned chorus girls attended by men either old, mustached, and rich or young, harried, and emaciated. At first I looked only at the sketches, but with age and diligence, I started understanding the captions.

The college bookstore was selling those same sensational books in the middle of the campus.

Within a couple of months I acquired in-depth knowledge of

paperback display racks and their contents through gainful employment at the bookstore. By happy chance I was placed in charge of stocking paperbacks!

Like other retail bookstores of the mid-1950s, this college store slowly and with some reluctance accepted mass market paperbacks and gradually increased its display space. The softcover display area increased more than tenfold in the four years I worked at the store. Management had discovered that paperbacks followed a basic rule of merchandising: the more displayed, the more sold.

I found that few of the books displayed were like the titles I had peeked at in Golden's Drugstore. At the time, it was customary for bookstores to arrange paperbacks according to publisher imprint. The "quality" paperback lines included Dover Books, Penguin and Pelican (dull-looking, but color-coded so that titles could be found more easily), Anchor, Vintage, and Meridian. All of these were good books, the kind that implied "read me for better grades." But then there were the others—"mass market paperbacks," I eventually learned to call them—books with illustrated covers from the publishers who also filled Golden's racks. Many were priced at only a quarter, but most were thirty-five cents and fifty cents, with a few big, bulky ones at seventy-five cents. A line of demarcation separated the top price of the cheap paperbacks and the ninety-five-cent bottom price of the "qualities."

The excesses of my drugstore adolescence were relived in that campus store. I spent countless hours arranging racks of Bantam roosters, Pocket Books kangaroos and cardinals, and Dell and Popular Library flora. I most enjoyed shelving the scarlet-stained Signet and Mentor paperbacks published by New American Library, which left me red-handed.

Nor was I the only bookstore employee so enchanted. The arrival of a shipment of new mass market releases was an event that the manager of the book department himself presided over. Packing knife in hand, he took great care not to slice the covers of the top layer of titles being premiered. The other student clerk and I eagerly awaited our turn for a look at the latest releases. Our critical attention was usually directed at the "big" titles metamorphosed into paperbacks. Often these were titles whose original highly touted hardcover edition had been returned unsold a few weeks earlier. We often discovered that the softcover edition would sell out within the week, however.

We also paid special attention to cover changes from previous editions; the books with reissued covers were almost always preferred to the earlier paperback issues, except for the price, which was often raised ten to fifteen cents. Without exception, our sales predictions at these grand openings were based more on the quality of the cover designs than on editorial content.

By clerking in that bookstore I learned that a particular title's sales were influenced not only by its own individual design but also by the designs of the books surrounding it in the display area. Some publishers' series had strong design formats, which worked to their sales advantage as long as booksellers shelved titles by publisher imprint. Strong designs—gold- or silver-spined Pocket Books and top- and bottom-banded designs such as Signet's—looked inviting when grouped together on a rack, but created a visual hodgepodge when mixed in a subject display with the formats of other publishers.

THE COVER RITUAL

Basic to a full appreciation of paperback cover art is an understanding of point of sale, the retail outlet—newsstand, supermarket, bookstore, or whatever—where paperback books are displayed for purchase. All the energies of a successful mass market paperback house are directed toward that outlet, the final sales link between the author's efforts and the reader's desire for information or entertainment. Point of sale is considered in all crucial decisions made by publishers, distributors, retailers, and even authors in marketing a particular title. These decisions invariably take into account not only the content of the book but also the manner in which the content is to be "packaged" for consumers.

In contemporary American mass market publishing there exists a mythology of beliefs surrounding the paperback cover. The adepts at the center of this mythology are the industry's art directors, key figures in the paperback publishing empires.

Each book project is a graphic ceremony, and the part that most fixes the attention of all concerned in the empire is the cover art. In preparation for the ceremony, the art director must ensure that all the traditions and formalities—the ideas of what a particular paperback "package" should contain—are properly observed in paperback "cover conferences," usually held six to eight months before the finished cover is produced.

Using the artwork as a base, the art director combines with it the other required design elements of the paperback format: author's name, book title, and editorial copy or "blurbs." Depending on the importance of the book, the art director may also throw in a few fancy wrinkles, like embossed figures, metallic foil, foldouts or step-backs, or die-cut peekaboos. With these innovations, borrowed from greeting cards, an art director sometimes can conjure up a blockbuster cover; other times he may lay an expensive egg.

And at whom are these efforts directed?—the middle-aged homemaker looking for escape reading in a suburban shopping center's bookstore, and her spouse heading home from work but delayed at a subway newsstand. Also, the retail and wholesale buyers who select books for these stores and newsstands, as well as the clerks and rackers who display the books for sale.

Few people in the industry claim to have an infallible understanding of the mysteries of cover art preparation and the formulas that ring up success. Daily, however, at each of the major mass market publishers the traditions and clichés that have governed cover art are repeated with much confidence in their effect. One aim of this book is to give the reader a clearer picture of the process of creating a design and an illustration for a paperback book.

THE INDUSTRY TODAY

Only recently has paperback book publishing gained recognition as an influential segment of the mass media. But even today its combined dollar income is only a fraction of the billions annually accumulated by corporate communications giants like CBS, MCA, and Warner, all of whom control one or more mass market lines. None of the conglomerates that currently own publishing houses started its subsidiary; all were acquired through merger. Frequently, however, after a publisher is subsumed into a larger corporate enterprise, a shakedown period follows, during which the paperback house establishes new identities and sales objectives for its imprints. A paperback *publisher* is the overall sponsoring agency for various paperback *imprints*. Thus, New American Library is publisher of the Signet Books imprint. Signet Classics are a *series* within the Signet imprint. New American Library is owned, however, by the Times Mirror Company of Los Angeles, a large *corporate* holding company.

Paperback book publishing's influence on the mass media is directly related to its product, the marketing of its product, and the adaptation of its product by the other mass media. The product, a book, is frequently used as the basis for a profitable movie or television production. The reverse also frequently happens: A movie or television production is profitably turned into a book. The book and the movie or television production both reach for the same mass audience, and advertising budgets for the joint ventures of book publishers and film producers may run into the millions. Alchemic combinations of cooperative publicity, promotion, and public relations try to transmute words and images into the gold of mass recognition and its resulting revenues.

Some blockbuster properties have bestowed on a small but growing number of writers monetary wealth resulting from film options and reprint rights. For some there is instant worldwide recognition: Norman Mailer, James Michener, Judith Krantz, Mario Puzo, Rosemary Rogers, Erich Segal, Irwin Shaw, and John Jakes, by virtue of their huge bestselling paperbacks, are now pop culture heroes.

Huge movie and television incomes, phenomena of the 1970s, have changed the face of twentieth-century general book publishing. Today, hardcover publishers are frequently accused of issuing particular books for the sole purpose of gaining substantial advances from softcover publishers—not of selling the books themselves. A sizable paperback sale can generate still more income through the attention the softcover edition captures from television and film producers. In recent years the sale of softcover reprint rights has frequently been sufficient to generate a television or movie purchase before a hardcover edition is even published. One publishing executive summed up this mass media partnership when he told *The New York Times:* "The future of the paperback lies in show biz."

This pivotal role of mass market publishing is a reversal of the original relationship that existed between hardcover publishers and paperback houses. When paperback publishers became established in mid-century, they were regarded solely as reprinters of successful titles first issued by hardcover houses and, therefore, dependent on hardcover publishers for their editorial material. Hardcover publishers controlled the proven and potential bestselling properties, frequently offering them to magazines, newspapers, and book clubs, and even hardcover reprinters, before paperback publishers were asked to bid. This was considered the natural order of things. Some paperback houses recognized the hardcover dominance by placing a photograph of the original hardcover version on their back cover, and in other ways encouraged readers to buy the hardcover for their permanent book collections. Until the Gold Medal imprint was established by Fawcett in 1949, little original material appeared initially in paperback.

By the late 1950s, however, the success of original publication series put mass market publishers in competition with hardcover houses for new writing talent. Established authors also found financial advantages in placing a manuscript first with a paperback house and then having a hardcover house acquire hardcover rights for first publication from the softcover publisher. In the 1950s, for example, John Faulkner, younger brother of William, left his hardcover publisher to write seven "backwoods" novels for Gold Medal. The most celebrated defection of a bestselling writer was Harold Robbins's departure in 1961 from Knopf to go to Pocket Books, which created its own hardcover imprint, Trident Press, to lure him. As this trend began taking shape, an English observer predicted, "The softcover publishers in America will be the bosses. They will commission the books and sign up the authors and they will decide whether they wish to give a license [to publish] to a hardcover publisher." Today, this is increasingly common in American trade-book publishing. Most paperback houses have under contract a profitable stable of bestselling writers and compete with hardcover houses for fresh writing talent.

The distinctions, therefore, that exist today between mass market paperback publishers and general hardcover publishers are blurry, often of degree rather than kind. The larger hardcover and paperback houses use the same basic publishing methods and sponsor the same broad range of editorial material. A large paperback publisher does issue much more category fiction and, of course, still publishes a large percentage of softcover reprints that follow initial hardcover publication. Both kinds of houses, however, publish trade paperbacks of various sizes and shapes. These are frequently aimed at special audiences and sold, like hardcover titles, almost exclusively through retail bookstores. And some of the major mass market houses have their own original hardcover book lines.

Hardcover publishers, in turn, have studied the mass-merchandising techniques of the paperback houses and have applied them successfully to their own publications. Witness Random House's success with James Michener's *Chesapeake*. With advertising and promotional hype lifted from the paperback bag, the book became an instant and durable hardcover bestseller in 1978 and 1979.

Still, there are paperback publishers today, as in the 1940s and 1950s, who are rightly labeled *mass market* paperback publishers. Contemporary American mass market paperback books, on which this survey focuses, are not only published in softcover but, most important, are physically designed, if not always written, for a mass audience and distributed with methods akin to magazine sales. Pocket Books, Avon, Dell, Bantam, New American Library, Fawcett, Ace, Ballantine, Popular Library, Berkley, Jove, and Warner are major mass market houses. All base their success on the distribution of a wide range of titles, in rack-size, softcover format, which are printed at high speed in quantities usually exceeding 100,000 copies. These publications are issued in monthly blocks, and 50 percent or more are sold to some 450 independent wholesale distributors for resale in more than 150,000 retail outlets across the United States and Canada.

My intent is to illustrate with words and pictures the basic features of American mass market publishing, from its beginnings in the nineteenth century through today, with a focus on the cover art and design. The key aspect of the paperback package, the cover design, symbolizes for reader, writer, and publisher the mass market paperback book industry as a whole. I emphasize the early years of contemporary paperback publishing in the United States, 1939–56, the time when most of the major softcover houses existing today were established. The reader will find lots of white space in my design. The industry has become the most dynamic section of American publishing, and, in a book of this scope, is too complex to render in any but the broadest way.

PART I
A Brief History

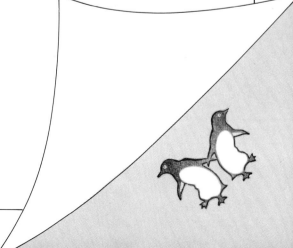

1
European Origins, American Roots

Throughout the nineteenth century in the United States, England, France, and Germany, numerous paperback series flourished: penny dreadfuls, yellowbacks, dime novels, cheap libraries, and the German *colporteur* novels. The Tauchnitz English-language Continental editions were nineteenth-century publications from which we can trace an unbroken lineage to contemporary American paperback publishing. Beginning in 1841 with Bulwer-Lytton's *Pelham,* Baron Christian B. von Tauchnitz distributed softcover editions of the works of British and American authors across Europe from his offices in Leipzig, Germany. Most titles were reprints, but occasionally they were used simultaneously with hardcover English and American editions. Unlike other foreign reprinters Tauchnitz paid fees for publication to English-language authors and their original publishers, thereby contributing to the eventual passage of nineteenth-century copyright laws. Both British and American writers considered it a great honor to be selected for inclusion in the Tauchnitz paperback series. Each Tauchnitz book was pocket-size, measuring roughly 4½″ × 6½″, and sold for approximately thirty-eight cents.

Historians of the book industry have identified the classics of Greek and Roman literature issued at the start of the sixteenth century by Venetian publisher and printer Aldus Manutius—the Aldine classics—as the earliest ancestors of today's paperbacks. Intended for students and scholars, they were small volumes

TAUCHNITZ AND ALBATROSS

An Aldine Classic edition (1528, measuring 3⅝″ x 6¼″) from a series that has been described as the "Bantams of their age." They were valued for their size, cheapness, and scholarship.

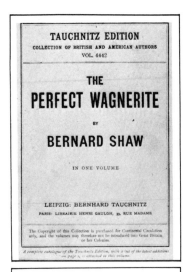

Distinguished English-language paperback editions issued for sale only on the European continent.
TOP: Tauchnitz (1913, 4⅝″ x 6⁷/₁₆″)
ABOVE: Albatross (1936, 4⅜″ x 7⅛″).

(roughly 5¾″ × 8″), well designed, and inexpensive. While some were original editions of previously unpublished manuscripts, most were fresh, authoritative translations of ancient writers. The Aldine classics were widely imitated and even counterfeited. Four hundred fifty years later their handsome anchor and dolphin printer's mark inspired the logo of one of the first American *trade* paperback series, Anchor Books. Straight typographic cover designs were used. European traditions encouraged owners either to dispose of them after reading or to rebind them for a permanent place in their libraries.

The Tauchnitz editions' most formidable rival for the European English-language trade, Albatross Books, was founded in 1931. A multinational operation, Albatross (a word common to most Western European languages) was a partnership of English and German publishers. Offices were located in Paris, London, and Hamburg; it was incorporated in Luxembourg, while distribution offices were located in Amsterdam, Bologna, Paris, and Leipzig. In 1934 Albatross acquired the Tauchnitz imprint and approximately five thousand Tauchnitz titles, the cream of one hundred years of British and American literature. One of the original partners in Albatross Books, Kurt Enoch, later managed the American Penguin branch and eventually cofounded in New York the New American Library, one of the largest of today's mass market houses.

Hans Mardersteig, considered by many to be the twentieth century's most prominent book designer, created a format for Albatross Books whose various elements continue to be adapted by softcover publishers to this day. His typographic cover design, with its multiple rectangular borders, was clean and classical. Jackets identical to the covers were wrapped around the volumes, and the book jackets and covers were color-coded. Genre identification was noted on the back flap of the dust jacket in Italian, French, Spanish, and English:

blue:	love stories
green:	stories of travel and foreign people
gray:	plays, poetry, and collected works
orange:	tales, short stories, and humorous and satirical works

purple: biographies and historical works
red: stories of adventure and crime
silver: anthologies
yellow: psychological novels, essays, and miscellaneous
          titles

A gliding-albatross logo appeared across both the front and unadorned back cover and jacket. The books stood 7⅛″ tall and approximately 4¼″ wide; these measurements provided a prototype for the basic mass market size. Adopted by Penguin and subsequently imported into the United States, it became by the early 1960s the standard for all major American mass market publishers.

Suppressed by the Nazis during World War II, both the Tauchnitz and Albatross imprints had brief rebirths during the postwar period.

A typical early Penguin (1935, 4⅜″ x 7⅛″), plainly designed but immediately recognizable.

In 1935, Allen Lane began publishing Penguin paperbacks in England. He had not only the Albatross design for a guide but, for better or worse, the example of nineteenth-century English softcover ventures as well. The checkered history and reputation of paperback forms, like the yellowbacks and penny dreadfuls, encouraged most people in the English book trade to vilify the impending flock of Penguins and predict their early extinction. However, when the English Woolworth chain agreed to carry the books, which sold for sixpence (about twelve cents), a conduit to the British reading public was opened wide and the future of the imprint was assured.

Moody and mercurial, Allen Lane was a shrewd businessman with a feel for both great literature and solid contemporary writing. Like Albatross, the Penguin imprint was color-coded, a practice that continues to this day. For more than twenty-five years Lane pointedly refrained from putting elaborate artwork on his covers; however, he was quick to point out that when the title suggested it, Penguin book covers allowed for some illustration. In the early 1960s, more elaborately illustrated covers began to appear on Penguin titles. Today very few Penguin fiction titles appear without some cover illustration.

PENGUIN BOOKS

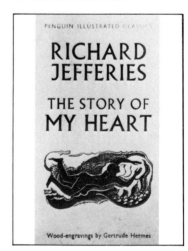

A rare instance of an early illustrated Penguin cover, part of a series of ten titles all published in May 1938.

European Origins, American Roots

27

Pirated 1842 editions of Dickens's
American Notes, both claiming to be
"firsts." TOP: *Brother Jonathan*
(roughly 8¼″ x 12⅜″). ABOVE:
The New World (roughly
7½″ x 11¹¹/₁₆″).

A Brief History

There are scattered examples of paper-wrapped books published in the United States before 1800, but these were not designed for mass distribution. It was an English series of the early nineteenth century, the Library of Useful Knowledge, which covered academic topics such as history, geography, mathematics, biology, and physics, and practical crafts such as husbandry, brewing, navigation, and iron manufacture, that inspired the first mass-produced books in America. Sponsored by the Boston Society for the Diffusion of Knowledge, the American Library of Knowledge began publication in 1831. These volumes were not softcover, but their 4″ × 6⅜″ dimensions closely matched today's duodecimo (roughly 4¼″ × 7⅛″) pocket-size volumes. Printed on quality book paper, they were well designed and, depending on the topic, usually well illustrated. The volumes were sold through bookstores and were priced at 62½ cents each. Although physically they may have been the forerunner of today's paperbacks, their editorial scope was similar to the English series that inspired them.

In July 1841 the first volume of *Charles O'Malley* was issued as a fifty-cent "extra" by *New World* literary magazine editor Park Benjamin. He and his colleagues at *New World* specialized in publishing American and pirated English and European writers in serial form and adopted the motto "The greatest good to the greatest number." *Brother Jonathan,* a rival literary weekly that Benjamin had earlier helped found, quickly followed the lead of *New World* by also sponsoring book supplements. Both magazines sold books through the mail and on the streets; mail subscriptions were unbound and coverless. Like the literary journals themselves, they were designed to look like newspapers, to take advantage of lower postal rates. *Brother Jonathan* called its book supplements country editions and sold them at 12½ cents an issue or ten for a dollar. Newsstand editions of the supplements were stained and bound with yellow, illustrated covers. *New World* and *Brother Jonathan* published their extras in editions that averaged 25,000 copies.

Supported by advances in papermaking and the invention of the cylinder printing press, newspapers in New York, Boston, and Philadelphia began to imitate the success of the two literary magazines. These were joined by established book publishers seeking to protect their investment in foreign writers and capture mass sales; however, prices eventually dropped to a point where no publisher could make money. This, combined with an overabundance of unsold supplements and a decision in 1843 by the Post Office to impose higher mailing rates, put an early end to the first paperback "revolution" in the United States. It lasted less than four years.

Surviving this first of the so-called paperback revolutions was cheap, sensational, and ephemeral fiction put out by a variety of publishers. However, when the Beadle brothers introduced a new series a year before the outbreak of the Civil War, a new fictional format was coined—the "dime novel." At their birth an ad in the *New York Tribune* proclaimed "Books for the Million," marking the beginning of one of the best-loved imprints in American publishing, Beadle's Dime Novels.

The first title, *Malaeska,* was a reprint of an earlier magazine story, but most tales were written especially for one of the several dime-novel series. Writers, who received $75–$150 for each manuscript, told tales of Western expansion that featured real heroes like Buffalo Bill and Kit Carson, as well as the fictional adventures of the ever popular Deadwood Dick, Jumbo Joe, Gospel George, Rosebud Rob, Darky Dan (the "colored detective"), and Nobby Nick of Nevada. The Beadle publications and the many dime-novel imitators appeared in different sizes and shapes. Best remembered are the early 4½″ × 6½″, 96-page booklets whose three separate signature gatherings were sewn and wrapped with an orange paper cover of approximately the same weight as the text paper, with simple woodcut illustrations depicting an action scene from the story. The publishers recognized that the cuts were as important as the title and content in producing newsdealer sales; particularly successful illustrations were given new life by appearing on more than one title.

In 1874 the original orange covers were discarded when competition from other dime-novel publishers and new cheap paperback reprint "libraries" led to the design of the gaudily colored but eye-catching "illuminated" covers of the New Dime Novel series (see Plate 1).   Sales of Beadle dime novels and their com-

DIME NOVELS

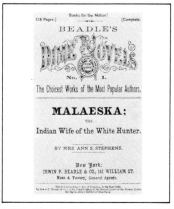

Beadle Dime Novels. TOP: First publication in the Beadle's Dime Novel series (1860, 4⅜″ × 6½″). ABOVE: Early reissue with an illustrated cover (4⅜″ × 6½″).

petitors declined through the 1880s and 1890s. The imprint changed hands in 1898 and again in 1905, but it continued to appear until 1937, a record of longevity unsurpassed by any other popular American publishing series.

THE LIBRARIES

Whereas dime-novel literature was generally limited to short, sensational fiction produced by American writers expressly for the inexpensive series, the publication in 1873 of two series of book supplements by the *New York Tribune* announced the return of paperback literature similar to that of the 1840s. European writers, still not protected from pirating in the United States, were again victimized by these editions. In the 1870s the introduction of ground-wood paper into bookmaking and even speedier printing presses supported this new wave of cheap publishing. These "library" editions cost a fourth to an eighth as much as hardcover titles and sold for as little as ten cents each. Low postage rates were also an inducement to these softcover libraries. Fourteen were in business in 1877, some started by publishers of dime novels.

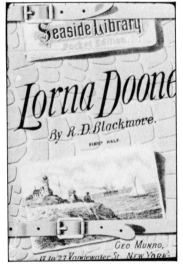

In this Seaside Library series the cover design was standard; only the author and title changed (1883, 4¾″ x 7⅛″).

Paperback library imprints stressed the leisure side of reading, beginning with the Lakeside Library and followed by Seaside Library, Riverside Library, and Fireside Library. Just as they had in the 1840s, established book publishers again entered the paperback ranks for survival. Joining the popular and serious American and European works in these paperback editions were ephemeral thrillers with titles like *Fatal Legacy, Red Revenger,* and *Wildlife in the West,* books little different from dime-novel literature. One-third of the 4,500 titles published in 1885 were paperbound, and cover prices dipped as low as five cents a volume. Like dime novels, these books were sold through the mails, individually and by subscriptions, as well as at newsstands and in established book shops.

These late-nineteenth-century examples of mass book production were first published in octavo size. In 1882, however, several publishers began to print editions in the more portable duodecimo or "cheap twelvemo" formats, sizes about a half inch wider and as tall as today's mass market paperbacks. In

A Brief History

30

fact, they were popularly called handy-size or pocket editions.

Early publications in these series generally had uniform typographic covers. Line drawings and two-, three-, and four-color cover illustrations followed. Romances often had cameo photographs on their front covers. By the late 1880s, few established writers had failed to appear in softcover, and many works were available in a variety of competing libraries.

By 1890 the quality of the physical paperback product reached new lows. Small type, bad printing, and cheap paper and binding were the norm. Cover art and copy became increasingly sensational, and pirating and wildcatting were commonplace. Worst was the great glut of books on the marketplace and their subsequent return to publisher warehouses: prices had to be slashed to the point of unprofitability. All this, combined with the new availability of inexpensive, cloth-covered books, signaled the recession of the paperback tide.

The second wave of paperback publishing in the United States finally ebbed in 1891, when, as publishing historian Frank Luther Mott has observed, "the pirates at last were forced to haul down their black flags" by the passage in Congress of the International Copyright Law. This legislation gave protection to foreign writers, provided their works were printed and published in the United States simultaneously with their appearance in their home countries.

Cheap paperback books never completely disappeared from the marketplace. However, the low editorial, production, and ethical standards of so many paperback publishers gave paperback books of the early twentieth century an unsavory image in the eyes of the public and booksellers alike. Few imprints survived the turn of the century. Most companies folded or sold their imprints and stock to competitors, some of whom lingered on for a decade or more. Street & Smith did continue to issue fiction in cheap paperbacks into the 1930s, with issues of some popular series appearing as often as once a week (see Plate 2), including tales of the ubiquitous detective Nick Carter and the success stories of Horatio Alger, Jr., both aimed at young readers. Clothbound reprints also flourished, including those of Grosset & Dunlap, a firm that in time became one of the most innovative and successful book publishers in the United States.

Long after the second paperback "revolution" reached its zenith, Street & Smith continued to issue cheap softcover books (circa 1914, 4⅝" x 6¹⁵/₁₆").

European Origins,
American Roots

LITTLE BLUE BOOKS Reminiscent of the publications of the London and Boston Useful Knowledge libraries of the early 1800s were the much-loved "Little Blue Books" of Kansas publisher Emanuel Haldeman-Julius. Aimed at spreading culture to the masses, his "University in Print" began publication in 1919. Included in the Little Blue Books series of more than two thousand titles were reprints of Shakespeare, Strindberg, Wilde, Verne, Twain, and Tolstoy, as well as original publications. A prolific writer as well as publisher, Haldeman-Julius's own prose and essays were listed with those of other faculty at his "university." The softcover booklets were generally sold at five cents a copy, though prices ranged between three cents and twenty-five cents.

The Blue Books measured 3½" × 5". After the first two years of publication, the books were issued in the format that made them famous, a plain blue typographic wrapper stapled around pages set in eight-point type. Although the imprint survived the death of its controversial and colorful founder in 1951, it lost the verve and impact it had possessed before World War II. Estimates credit the company with selling over 500 million booklets, mostly through the mails, before it ceased publication in 1964. Little Blue Books had proved that good literature, if made inexpensively available, could find a mass American market.

BONI If the Kansas-plain Little Blue Books were antidesign, Boni paperback volumes introduced in 1929 were quite the opposite. Roughly quarto size, the handsomely made softcover titles had sewn bindings wrapped with soft covers designed by some of the leading illustrators of the day. Rockwell Kent, for instance, designed and illustrated the early volumes in the Charles Boni Paper Books series. These were book-club editions and were sold on a subscription basis, twelve books a year for five dollars. Aimed at the retail trade was a second series, Boni Books, started in 1930 and priced at fifty cents.

In 1917 the Boni brothers, Charles and Albert, helped start the hardcover classics reprint series Modern Library, later to become a foundation stone of Bennett Cerf's Random House. In 1929, however, the Bonis were eager to make the paperback format respectable in public eyes. In an early publicity release, Charles stated: "I have always wanted to furnish the American public with paperbound books at low costs, in the form so successful and popular throughout Europe. . . . Only quality production will make it possible to publish good books, better printed than those now offered in cloth bindings, on equally good paper, at one-seventh of the current book price." In content, the books were equal to their quality packaging. They were selected by a distinguished editorial board to appeal to serious hardcover readers; authors included Thornton Wilder, Maxim Gorky, Herman Melville, Sherwood Anderson, and D. H. Lawrence.

The Boni brothers were uncertain about highbrow acceptance of the softcover format; therefore, a subscriber to the book club could return a volume and, for one dollar, have it encased in a Rockwell Kent-designed cloth binding. A cloth binder device was also offered to those who wished to add respectability to their paper edition.

Like so many ventures started in the late 1920s, both paperback series sank with the economy: in 1931 the Bonis ceased reprinting softcover titles. In the experience of the Bonis, however, the title selection and designs of today's trade paperback books are strongly foreshadowed.

An immediate precursor of both Pocket Books and the trade paperback imprints of the 1950s. A Boni paperback illustrated by Rockwell Kent (1930, 4⅞″ x 7⅜″).

The most interesting pre-1939 experiment in paperback book publishing, however, was Modern Age Books. During its short life, from 1937 to 1942, this company employed the production, promotion, and marketing methods, including the use of wholesale magazine distributors, that would be successful for the mass market paperback houses of the 1940s and 1950s. One cause of the company's failure was its relatively uninspired editorial selection and the design of its physical format. The publisher failed to recognize that the mass market it wanted to attract was made up of people who were not regular book buyers. The titles tended to be literary; the books themselves were large (usually 5½″ × 7½″) and heavily bulked—a 300-page book was almost an inch thick. One can easily imagine these rather sedate, often two-color typographic covers running a poor second on newsstands to the homely appeal of a *Collier's* or *Saturday Evening Post* cover illustration, or the flash, flesh, and fantasy exploding on pulps

OTHER PRE-POCKET BOOKS IMPRINTS

European Origins, American Roots

Designed and illustrated by George Salter, this digest-sized publication was published by Lawrence E. Spivak (1944, 5⅜″ x 7⅝″).

such as *Amazing Stories* or *Spicy Detective,* which then were dominating the racks.

American Mercury Books, conceived by its publisher, Lawrence E. Spivak of *Meet the Press* fame, also began publication in 1937. This "digest-size" imprint was distributed by Select Magazines, a national periodical distributor, through many of the same mass market channels first used by Modern Age. Title selection differed greatly, however. American Mercury Books and successor imprints were extensions of the pulp-magazine literature then flourishing. Seldom was a title reprinted, and, like magazines, they were numbered and issued monthly. Displayed on the same racks, they complemented the digest magazines and murder monthlies that continue to be sold today. Nevertheless, the imprints of American Mercury of the 1940s and 1950s are distinguished for the work done by their cover artist and designer George Salter, who instructed and influenced many of today's book designers, illustrators, and calligraphers.

2
Pocket Books

The New *Pocket* Books that may revolutionize New York's
reading habits

On June 19, 1939, this headline for a full-page *New York Times*
ad announced Pocket Books' entry into book publishing. The ad
continued:

> Today is the most important literary coming-out party in
> the memory of New York's oldest book lover. Today your
> 25¢ piece leaps to a par with dollar bills.
>
> Now for less than the few cents you spend each week for
> your morning newspaper you can own one of the great
> books for which thousands of people have paid from $2 to
> $4.
>
> These new Pocket Books are designed to fit both the
> tempo of our times and the needs of New Yorkers. They're
> as handy as a pencil, as modern and convenient as a porta-
> ble radio—and as good looking. They were designed spe-
> cially for busy people—people who are continually on the
> go, yet who want to make the most of every minute.
>
> Never again need you say "I wish I had time to read"
> because Pocket Books gives you the time. Never again need
> you dawdle idly in reception rooms, fret on train or bus
> rides, sit vacantly staring at a restaurant table. The books

you have always meant to read "when you had time" will fill the waits with enjoyment.

Eighteen months before, Robert de Graff had left fourteen years of hardcover and reprint publishing to begin work on his fondest dream: "I am convinced that the mass American public wants the best in books . . . at irresistibly low prices, with almost universal distribution."

Robert de Graff studied the editorial selection of several paperback series as he groomed his own publication program. He was able to compare, for instance, the success of Penguin and Pelican in England with the mixed reception Modern Age received in the United States.

The Pocket Books venture became a certainty when Richard Simon, M. Lincoln Schuster, and Leon Shimkin of the Simon & Schuster Publishing Company agreed to buy a 49 percent interest in the fledgling company. De Graff ensured his personal control by retaining 51 percent. Backed by adequate capital, De Graff began to devise an array of mail promotions, which included descriptions of his publishing program and an experimental list of prospective titles, for which he solicited comments and orders. He also printed, sampled, and sold a 2,300-copy edition of Pearl Buck's *The Good Earth*. (A second edition later became the eleventh title on the Pocket Books list.)

BALANCING A LIST   De Graff was still experimenting with title selection when he issued his first ten titles in 1939. They were a mixed bag of books that had enjoyed modest to great success in hardcover and represented a wide range of literature: bestseller fiction, comedy, drama, poetry, mystery, juvenile fiction, self-help, and classics.

The first ten books, published in June 1939, were:
1. *Lost Horizon* by James Hilton
2. *Wake Up and Live!* by Dorothea Brande
3. *Five Great Tragedies* by William Shakespeare
4. *Topper* by Thorne Smith
5. *The Murder of Roger Ackroyd* by Agatha Christie
6. *Enough Rope* by Dorothy Parker
7. *Wuthering Heights* by Emily Brontë
8. *The Way of All Flesh* by Samuel Butler

ABOVE LEFT: Pocket Books, sample edition (November 1938, 4⅛″ x 6½″).

ABOVE RIGHT: No. 11 edition (August 1939).

I am always glad when any of my books can be put into an inexpensive edition, because I like to think that any people who might wish to read them can do so. Surely books ought to be within the reach of everybody.

Pearl S. Buck

LEFT: The dedication that Pearl Buck wrote for the first Pocket Books edition.

Ten Pocket Books titles published in June 1939:

Illustrated by Isadore Steinberg.

Illustrated by Frank J. Lieberman.   Illustrated by Frank J. Lieberman.   Illustrated by Frank J. Lieberman.

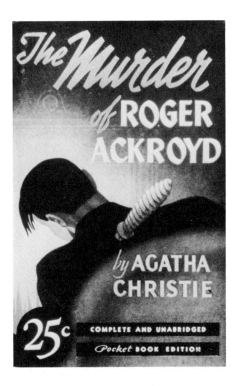

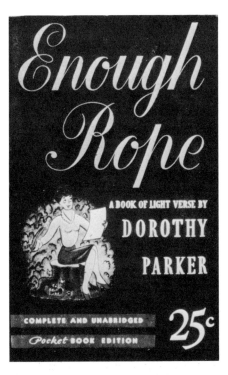

LEFT: Illustrator unknown.

RIGHT: Illustrated by Frank J. Lieberman.

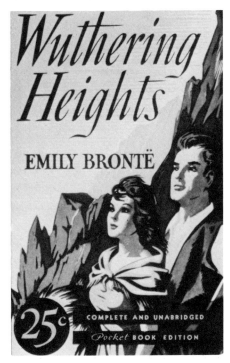

LEFT: Illustrated by Isadore Steinberg.

RIGHT: Illustrated by Isadore Steinberg.

9. *The Bridge of San Luis Rey* by Thornton Wilder
10. *Bambi* by Felix Salten

Besides the obvious attempt to cater to general literary taste with this eclectic selection, it is interesting to note that four of the ten were or soon would be motion pictures *(Lost Horizon, Topper, Wuthering Heights,* and *The Way of All Flesh).* Two film sequels to *Topper* were produced within the next two years, and by 1944, films were also made of the last two titles on this list.

De Graff quickly discovered that his first best seller was *Wuthering Heights,* and the reason was obvious: The recently released film starring Laurence Olivier and Merle Oberon had received wide acclaim. Dorothea Brande's self-help title, *Wake Up and Live!* achieved respectable, if not outstanding, sales, but later Pocket Books instructional books, *How to Win Friends and Influence People* by Dale Carnegie and Dr. Spock's *Baby and Child Care,* became publishing legends. The Shakespeare tragedies and *Bambi* were precursors of the classics and children's paperback series that would be established by publishers fifteen and twenty-five years later when marketing techniques were more refined, thus enabling them to target and reach specific audiences.

Topper, in addition to being filmed, represented the genre of humor that later became a staple of paperback lists, like classic and self-help titles. A Pocket Books edition of an army private's misadventures in boot camp, *See Here, Private Hargrove,* became the bestselling paperback of the wartime period.

No romances, Westerns, or science fiction appeared among the first ten titles; however, there was a mystery: Agatha Christie's classic work of detection *The Murder of Roger Ackroyd.* For the next few months, most of Pocket's subsequent lists of new titles also included a mystery. Yet De Graff was disappointed with their sales until he discovered a basic principle of publishing category books for the mass market: Like books shelved side by side attract readers of that type or category, and when enough are displayed together, they sell themselves, and generally at a predictable rate.

By June 1940, De Graff's monthly output reflected this marketing concept, and for many years about one-third of all Pocket titles were mysteries. Agatha Christie, represented on that first list, sold steadily and well through the next forty years, giving credence to the claim that she is the world's bestselling female writer. The mysteries of Erle Stanley Gardner also contributed greatly to the first twenty years of Pocket Books' success. Between 1941 and 1975, nineteen Pocket-produced Perry Mason bestsellers laid a solid publishing base for the company and achieved for Gardner the accolade of "the most widely sold writer in the world."

Approximately 10,000 copies of each of the first ten titles were printed, an insignificant number when measured against today's mass market first printings. Within a week the inventory was exhausted; second printings of 15,000 were immediately ordered. Four new titles were added in August, and by the end of 1939 approximately 1.5 million copies had been shipped.

Initially, traditional trade bookstores and department stores were seen as the chief outlets for paperbacks; however, a sizable first order was placed by a news company that owned street and subway newsstands throughout New York City. Soon, national drug- and cigar-store chains were carrying the books, as well as large variety-store chains. Sears, Roebuck and Spiegel agreed to include Pocket Books in their mail-order catalogs. Another breakthrough occurred when two of the nation's largest department-store buying offices reached a marketing agreement with Pocket. By the end of the first eighteen months of publication, however, Pocket Books had yet to reach the American mass reading audience.

Pocket Books' contributions to the successful growth of paperback publishing in the United States are legion, but chief among them is the method of distribution the company initiated in 1941. That year, Wallis "Pete" Howe, Pocket's first sales representative, returned from a spring sales trip with orders from four independent wholesale distributors (IDs) of magazines and tabloids. These IDs agreed to distribute Pocket Books to their newsstand, drugstore, grocery- and variety-store accounts. One of the early wholesale distributors recently recalled his quandary when initially called by a Pocket Books representative. He believed at first that the salesman was taking orders for wallets!

By year's end, however, most of the nation's 700 ID's knew

DISTRIBUTING A LIST

what Pocket Books were and had started distributing them to an estimated 100,000 retail outlets. True mass distribution had been achieved. *Time* magazine quickly recognized this accomplishment and the impact it would have on America. Using Columbus, Ohio, one of the first areas to receive ID paperback distribution, as an example, *Time* pointed out in May 1941 that six outlets existed in Columbus for hardcover books; however, Pocket Books were sold at 224 places in the same area. By 1949, Pocket Books could claim it had exceeded the combined unit sales of all the bestselling titles published in the United States since 1880.

Today, despite the significant growth of sophisticated jobber and retail bookstore-chain operations, local independent distributors represent at least 60 percent of all paperback sales and continue to be the major link of mass market publishers with today's reading public.

ESTABLISHMENT

The years of experience and planning that preceded the first Pocket Books list paid big dividends for the company during the early days of its existence. Through association with Simon & Schuster, Pocket Books quickly acquired respectability within the publishing industry, a respectability that most other softcover reprinters took many years to attain. This solid reputation eased the job of acquiring attractive bestselling titles. As a result, there was a high correlation between the 1939–49 bestseller lists and the Pocket Books lists of approximately the same period.

De Graff continued to emphasize popular fiction, mysteries, and self-help books. Movie tie-ins, either with or without the cooperation of the film producers, also continued to produce big sales. Taking a cue from magazine publishers, Pocket Books kept to a monthly schedule, which usually amounted to five new titles. Some months twice that number were issued, but during World War II new editions fell to four or less a month.

Early Pocket Books editorial selections, format design, and marketing methods reflected the company's belief that there were different audiences for the same book in its hardcover original, hardcover reprint, and paperback editions; therefore, paperback reprints would not harm sales of original editions. Further,

Pocket Books believed their audience comprised readers who wanted to buy books but simply did not have access to retail outlets for hardcover editions or could not afford them when they did. This same belief had inspired softcover reprint ventures in the 1930s. Gradually, however, a new perception of the mass book-reading audience evolved that included people who usually did not read books but were attracted to the flash and promise of the softcover format, people whose eyes had wandered from retail magazine displays to neighboring paperback racks.

In July 1940, Pocket Books ensured its success with the publication of Dale Carnegie's *How to Win Friends and Influence People*. At the time, it was the most successful self-help book ever to appear in American publishing. To every reader Carnegie offered:

> Six ways of making people like you.
> Twelve ways of winning people to your way of thinking.
> Nine ways to change people without giving offense or arousing resentment.
> Plus: Seven rules for making your home life happier.

How could it miss? Because the Carnegie book was a staple of Simon & Schuster's hardcover list, De Graff had to convince the managers of Simon & Schuster that his paperback sales would not harm their hardcover profits. He suggested doing a market test in Texas. Years later chief salesman Pete Howe observed that "the canny De Graff" was aware that Texas had the biggest concentration of drug chains in the country and that their leading distributor was a drug-chain sales agency. One of Pocket Books' largest accounts, the national chain of Kress five-and-ten-cent chain stores, also concentrated their business in Texas. Howe recalled the pitch De Graff made to the three S & S partners, Simon, Schuster, and Shimkin:

> De Graff opened his big blue eyes and I kind of felt sorry for the three Esses because they didn't know what was about to hit them. "I don't want you fellows to take any risk whatsoever, so let's make a test. We'll take the toughest sales area in the country—Texas. . . . We can hardly hope to win, but I think we owe it to you."

Third printing, 1940, with individually printed edition serial numbers.

Pocket Books

43

Following the very successful test in Texas, distribution was extended across the country, and sales of the Carnegie reprint doubled the income received from the rest of Pocket's list. It was reprinted five times by November 1940.

When World War II broke out, the company was in good financial shape and able to absorb the shock of inflation, paper shortages, and loss of publishing talent. The problem of over-supply and book returns, that congenital infirmity of mass-distributed books, did not reach significant proportions until immediately after World War II. During the war almost everything printed was sold either through regular distribution channels or through special bulk sales worked out with the branches of the armed services.

DE GRAFF IN RETROSPECT

With Pocket Books, Robert de Graff solved the dilemma presented in 1932 to American publishers in the well-known Chaney Report on the state of American book publishing: "At this point the publisher has books; at that point is the book buyer. Between these two points is the tragedy of the book industry."

By 1939 all of the elements that were to contribute to the successful marketing of mass market paperback books had been attempted in one or more different editorial, design, production, and distribution combinations, both in the United States and in Europe.

Editorially, the books had to attract an audience that did not frequent traditional retail bookstores. The kind of literature that would appeal to this audience was known from the paperback waves of the nineteenth century and the mass magazines of the twentieth. Eventually, publishers refined their categories of readers to the point that genres such as mysteries, romances, Westerns, and science fiction gave birth to numerous subcategories.

In 1939 publishers still believed that the notoriety attendant on hardcover publication—publicity, reviews, word-of-mouth recommendations—was necessary before a paperback edition could succeed, yet original paper editions had been published continuously throughout the second half of the nineteenth century and by Street & Smith in the twentieth.

In the years preceding the advent of Pocket Books, high-speed rotary magazine presses had been used to print paperbacks in quantities sufficient to permit cover prices of twenty-five cents or less. Six years after World War II specially designed rubber-plate presses were imported from England for even greater efficiency. The rack-size book dimensions that outlined the boundaries of a portable book package could trace their roots to sixteenth-century Europe. The appeal of color illustration on the cover of paperbacks was known for more than seventy-five years.

Distribution systems designed to place reading material in various types of retail outlets—newsstands, drug, chain, and variety stores—were almost one hundred years old in 1939. Molding and refining these systems, which also distribute magazines, comics, and newspapers, continues to be the constant concern of today's mass market publishers.

But not until Robert de Graff merged his ideas for Pocket Books with the solid marketing experience and financial resources of Simon & Schuster were these major elements combined in a way that ensured the survival and growth of paperbacks. More than any other individual, De Graff must be credited with establishing the methods and directions taken by contemporary paperback book publishing. Through trial and error, success and failure, he and Pocket Books provided a solid base around which other prosperous paperback houses patterned their operations. During World War II and in the years immediately following, De Graff's curious mixture of idealism, business perception, and enlightened self-interest provided leadership in the field of mass reading and gave the paperback reprint industry a respect it had never enjoyed before in the United States. Much of this respect was subsequently lost when the sensational paperback "literature" and covers of the late 1940s and early 1950s dominated newsstands and America's image of what was contained in paperback books. Robert de Graff's contributions, however, remain untarnished.

Robert de Graff and friend.

3
Early Childhood of an Industry

One month after Robert de Graff issued his first list of books, Ian Ballantine, an American student studying in England, returned to the United States in the employ of Allen Lane, the founder of Penguin Books. Ballantine was to establish a branch office in New York to import and distribute the English softcover imprint. It quickly became clear, however, that the import difficulties resulting from World War II called for a separate publishing program, and by the fall of 1940 Penguins were being manufactured in the United States. Ballantine was joined in 1941 by Kurt Enoch, a cofounder of Albatross Books and a refugee from Nazi oppression in Europe. Lane asked Enoch to assist Ballantine with the production aspects of the business and to raise money so that the American branch could be financially independent of London. By the following year the American branch had reversed the original pattern of distribution: it was exporting American-made Penguins to England.

The first American paperback house to appear after the start of Pocket Books was Red Arrow Books. This series was first published in the latter part of 1939 by Columbia Art Works, Inc., a Milwaukee offset printer. The first Red Arrows had typographic covers and, like Albatross and Penguin, were color-coded by type of literature. However, reissues appeared with illustrated covers, leading to speculation that the design was directly influenced by Pocket Books' early success. The imprint lasted only about a year.

With financial backing from the American News Company, Joseph Meyers organized Avon Books in the fall of 1941. Avon was the first serious challenge to Pocket Books' almost exclusive control of cheap reprint book sales. Pocket Books took Avon to court in 1942, charging that Avon's design was so similar to Pocket Books' that people could be deceived into buying an Avon title when it was a Pocket Book they were after. Following two offsetting court decisions, Avon came away victorious in 1944. The New York State Court of Appeals ruled that despite obvious similarities in size and design, Avon's Shakespeare-bust logo and the legend "AVON pocket-size BOOKS" were sufficient to allow readers to distinguish between Avon and Pocket Books. (See Plate 3.) By this time, however, Avon had dropped "pocket-size" from its legend.

Popular Library and Dell Books, both spinoffs of magazine publishers, were issuing paperbacks by 1943 (see Plates 4a and b). Each developed a list of outstanding mystery, detective, and Western titles, which reflected their magazine successes. Dell also published many romances, a category particularly favored by the guiding hand of the book program, Helen Meyer. Distributed by Dell, and carrying a distinctive keyhole logo, the list was edited, designed, and printed by Western Publishing Company (then known as Western Printing and Lithographing). For approximately eight years Dell books had an illustration on the back cover depicting a principal scene or location in the book. Today these Dell mapbacks are much sought after by collectors of vintage paperbacks. (See Plates 29a–d.)

The end of World War II marked a time of great expansion in the paperback industry. Returning soldiers and sailors carried home memories and tattered copies of the Armed Services Editions, reprints issued especially for them during the war. As the Beadles had experienced eighty years before, a new reading audience was created by a greatly enlarged army and navy. During World War II soldiers and sailors found cheap paperback reprints a means to escape tedium or loneliness. The ubiquitous Armed Services Editions were widely available to them. Robert de Graff served on the board of the Council on Books in Wartime, which gave general direction to this government-financed publishing project.

Paperback historian Frank Schick has observed:

Variant editions of the same Red Arrow title published in 1939 or 1940. This book was also selected by Dell as the first title in their paperback series. (See also Plate 4a.)

Early Childhood of an Industry

A total of 1,324 titles were published in "Armed Services Editions," of which only ninety-nine had previously been reprinted. They were a bargain for the government, which bought 123.5 million copies at an average cost of 6.09¢ per volume before the project ended in 1946. The men in the services who got them free of charge welcomed them enthusiastically. Never before had so many books at such a low price found such a large number of avid readers.

Designed to be portable (they fit comfortably into the pocket of an army fatigue jacket) and disposable, they were trimmed to half the size of *The Reader's Digest* or other contemporary pulp magazines.

LATER COMPETITORS

The same title in Pocket Books (1946) and Armed Services Editions (1943). The latter series generally came in two sizes, 3¹³/₁₆" x 5½" (shown here) and 4½" x 6⁷/₁₆".

In 1945 Bantam Books entered the softcover marketplace with a list aimed at competing head to head with Pocket Books, the acknowledged leader in the paperback field. Editorial and distribution policy differences with Allen Lane had caused Ian Ballantine to leave the New York office of Penguin Books and, with key members of the branch, to organize and direct Bantam. Bantam had the financial backing of the Curtis Publishing Company, publishers and distributors of the very successful mass-circulation slick magazines *The Saturday Evening Post* and the *Ladies' Home Journal,* and of Grosset & Dunlap, the hardcover reprinter, which had recently been acquired by a consortium of trade-book publishers: Random House, Harper's, Charles Scribner's Sons, Little, Brown, and the Book-of-the-Month Club.

Ballantine obtained reprint rights to Hemingway, Steinbeck, and Fitzgerald, writers who were then achieving worldwide recognition. From this solid beginning, Bantam went on to become the dominant paperback publisher of the 1960s and 1970s.

Meanwhile, at Penguin one of the most dynamic partnerships in the history of American publishing was taking root. Victor Weybright, who had become acquainted with Allen Lane while stationed in England during the war, joined Kurt Enoch at the American branch of Penguin. By late 1947, Enoch and Weybright's differences with Penguin of England led them to negotiate an agreement with Lane whereby they acquired the rights to Penguin and Pelican titles originally sponsored for reprint by the American branch. Enoch and Weybright incorporated their company as the New American Library of World Literature (NAL) and established two landmark imprints, Signet and Mentor. Harking back to late-nineteenth-century softcover publisher slogans, the legend "Good Reading for the Millions" appeared on all their new publications.

NAL's first publication in the spring of 1948, Faulkner's *The Wild Palms,* is indicative of the quality of fiction that editor-in-chief Weybright sought for reprinting. The backwoods literature of Erskine Caldwell and the pseudo-sadistic detective novels of Mickey Spillane also achieved record sales during NAL's early years, placing it by the mid-1950s in direct competition with Pocket Books for the title of largest paperback publisher.

At this time, Fawcett Publications was a leading publisher of popular magazines, including *True, True Confessions,* and *Mechanix Illustrated.* Fawcett also served as the national agency for the sale of Signet and Mentor paperbacks to independent wholesalers across the United States and Canada. Their contract with NAL specifically prohibited Fawcett from issuing their own *reprints* of hardcover works; however, the contract did not rule out original publishing.

Up to this time Pocket Books, NAL, and other softcover publishers had only occasionally issued original material, mainly anthologies that did not threaten the delicate balance struck between original hardcover publishers and paperback reprinters. This balance actually meant that paperback houses bowed to hardcover houses in the acquisition of new writing talent. In the spring of 1950 Fawcett upset the equilibrium by starting a full-scale original publishing program.

Hardcover and established softcover publishers expressed grave concern over this breach of the gentleman's agreement and theorized on its implications. There was less theorizing on the part of writers. It was clear that the average novelist would come out better financially contracting with Fawcett. The writer received an immediate three-thousand-dollar advance rather than having to wait for hardcover royalties that seldom exceeded two thousand dollars after publication. One young author, whose hardcover edition disappeared without a trace soon after publication, observed another advantage of the softer format, "A paper cover floats better."

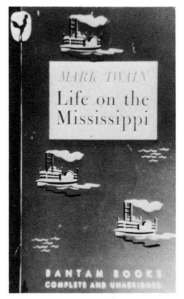

Bantam Book No. 1 (1945). Illustrated by H. Lawrence Hoffman.

A period of transition. For a few months in 1948 newly published New American Library titles carried dual imprints. Both covers illustrated by Robert Jonas.

A chain reaction began within the publishing industry, and other paperback houses, including Dell, Avon, and Popular Library, soon followed suit. By 1955 one-third of all mass market titles issued were originals.

Fawcett's Gold Medal imprint has been responsible for publishing original works by some of America's most widely read writers of fiction, including John D. MacDonald, Taylor Caldwell, and Mackinlay Kantor. The bulk of Fawcett's early offerings, however, were potboilers, condemned to obscurity immediately after publication. These books once prompted Bernard De Voto, sharp-tongued critic of the fifties' literary scene, to declare: "What Gold Medal has proved is we didn't know how lousy novels could be."

In 1952, Ian Ballantine left Bantam to start yet another paperback publishing operation, Ballantine Books. He aimed to satisfy both writers and hardcover publishers. To authors he offered advances that averaged five thousand dollars, and he guaranteed both hard- and softcover publication. Ballantine sought out hardcover publishers who were willing to copublish hardcover editions simultaneously with his softcover editions. Production costs of both were to be reduced by using the same printing plates. The advantages to the hardcover publisher were guaranteed royalties from paperback sales and reduced manufacturing costs on their own hardcover editions. But the idea never received widespread support among hardcover publishers, with only two houses giving full cooperation. Ballantine did sponsor several hardcover works of his own and is noted for being the first mass market publisher to issue his own original hardcover imprint.

The Gold Medal and Ballantine experiments of the early 1950s had the immediate effect of changing the attitudes of both writers and publishers. Authors began to look not only for better royalty arrangements from hardcover publishers but also for guarantees of publication in softcover. Writers, known and unknown, started placing their manuscripts with mass market houses. Paperback houses in turn began to offer these same manuscripts to hardcover houses while retaining paperback rights. Thus paperback publishers were able to build up stables of their own authors.

By the early 1950s the major paperback publishers—and major

operating patterns that were to be followed for the next thirty years—were established. Included were several companies that contributed to the ever growing strength of softcover publishing.

Ace Books, by introducing thirty-five-cent double novels in 1952, used a gimmick that every paperback publisher has probably tried at one time or another: publication of two or more books in one binding (see Plate 5). Westerns, mysteries, and science fiction made up the bulk of Ace's offerings. Publication of the double novels ceased in the 1960s; however, the books, which have two front covers, and, therefore, two pieces of cover art, are hoarded by today's paperback collectors. Two other paperback publishers of note began publication at this time: Pyramid Books, started by the Almat Publishing Corporation in 1949, and Berkley Books, founded in 1954.

With few exceptions, most of the paperback publishers who followed Pocket Books in the 1940s and 1950s had extensive experience in the magazine business, as opposed to the book business. Dell and Fawcett were among the largest periodical publishers in the country when they began their book programs. Ace, Avon, Berkley, Popular Library, and Pyramid all were directed by men with mass-circulation magazine experience. Harvey Swados, observing the publishing scene in 1951, remarked, "Magazine publishers were the logical people to jump into a new operation requiring considerable capital, mass production, wide distribution, and a rapid rate of sale in a market where space is at a premium and competition compels the replacement of titles as rapidly as of periodicals."

Ballantine No. 1 (1952). Illustrated by Harry Bennett.

4
Challenges for an Industry

The 1940s and 1950s were littered with the remains of numerous mass market publishers, many of them offshoots of magazine and magazine-distributing companies that did not survive the competition. Among them were Lion Library, Graphic, Bart House, Anson Bond, Hillman, Handi, Black Knight, and, appropriately enough, Bleak House. Those companies that had achieved solid commercial success by dominating the paperback racks in the 1950s did so by following the same publishing patterns that Robert de Graff established in the early 1940s: broad editorial selection; attractive design; cheap, high-speed manufacture; and distribution through local wholesale channels. By the early 1950s, when Fawcett and Dell began to publish quantities of original fiction, all of the major elements that contributed to the success of the American mass market book industry were in place. It remained for each publisher to deal individually or collectively with a variety of operational problems, including cover prices, book returns, and censorship.

COVER PRICES "I still think of a good book as twenty-five cents," remarked one recently retired founder of a softcover house. In the 1940s and most of the 1950s, paperback books and their twenty-five-cent cover price were synonymous. Some publishers did not even print the retail price on their books: everyone knew that paperbacks sold for a quarter, just as a package of gum sold for a nickel. This situation lasted for as long as publishers could produce a book for substantially less than twenty-five cents.

After the war, however, inflation in general and the cost of paper in particular caused publishers to cheapen their packaging to maintain the twenty-five-cent price. Shorter works were published more often than longer books because less paper was needed to print them. Longer works, when published, were often abridged: Shakespeare's *Five Great Tragedies,* Pocket Books #3, became *Four Great Tragedies* in 1948. Page designs returned to the cramped standards of World War II. Protective cover laminations were dropped and replaced with covers sprayed with a coat of varnish.

In the late 1940s, NAL's Mentor series and Doubleday's Permabooks sold for thirty-five cents, but most publishers entered the 1950s very reluctant to break the twenty-five-cent price barrier. By the mid-1950s, however, economics forced them to establish thirty-five-cent publications as well. There was little buyer resistance to the thirty-five-cent price. A reader could successfully accept the 1956 newspaper invitation of Brentano's Fifth Avenue store to visit their new paperback book department and, for ten dollars, walk out with a whole library. Throughout the history of modern mass market publishing, various perceived price barriers have been approached and eventually overcome. Barriers of one, two, and three dollars were breached in the early 1960s, mid-1970s, and late 1970s respectively. In 1979 the *average* price of a mass market paperback had risen to $2.06, more than double the average of ninety-three cents reported ten years earlier. Clearly, ten dollars today will not fill a small paper bag with softcover books. There is much concern among publishers over statistics showing that in recent years, while the dollar income of the industry has increased, the number of copies sold has essentially remained the same—a possible indication that paperback readership may be declining.

Since ancient times unsold publications have been a problem for publishers. Two thousand years ago the Roman poet Martial observed: "Remainders were sold to tradesmen for wrapping paper or went to feed the worms." The latter fate was common for unsold paperbacks in the late 1940s and early 1950s. Hundreds of

RETURNS

Challenges for
an Industry

thousands of copies were dumped in landfills. These inventories tie up working capital, choke the channels of distribution, and threaten publishers with the same financial ruin that nineteenth-century softcover imprints experienced.

Since the mid-1950s, most mass market publishers have not taken back whole books for credit from their major accounts. Instead, a practice similar to that used by the magazine industry is employed. Publishers receive only the front cover of their publication and require the credited account to destroy the remainder of the book. Approximately 90 percent of mass market returns are in the form of "stripped" books. Coverless books that do not get destroyed have become a concern to the paperback industry because they are the basis for illegal stripped-book sales, which flourish in certain parts of the United States.

In 1980, approximately 423 new paperback printings appeared each month. Except for large general bookstore accounts, few retail stores have enough display space to accept more than 50 percent of this monthly output; most receive much less. The vast majority of returned paperbacks are editions only a few months old. Today, an "acceptable" rate of book return is considered 35 percent; for many companies, however, the rate is much higher, exceeding 50 percent or more. Over 100 million paperbacks are destroyed annually.

Perhaps the most successful of the many approaches publishers have taken to cope with oversupply and returns is to develop strong backlist programs. Backlist titles are generally books that were successful in generating reorders from retailers fairly soon after publication and are likely to continue to inspire new orders for an indefinite period of time. A publisher will usually keep a title in print and on the backlist as long as the edition's future predicted sales are deemed sufficient to justify a new printing each time stock runs out. Because they are ordered by book buyers to fill a specific need or as a result of successful past sales, returns from backlist orders are relatively small. Authors, too, are pleased with paperback houses that keep their works in print. "Better read than dead" has more than once summarized this point of view.

"Making a publisher eat" is a phrase booksellers use to describe the balancing of publisher accounts when they return books for credit instead of cash. Rather than nourishment, however, this legacy of the nineteenth century is the recurring disease of the mass market paperback industry, a sickness that destroys perhaps as many as one out of every three softcover books printed, a sickness that cries out to be controlled but probably will never be eliminated.

In several different senses the most visible problem that confronted the paperback industry, particularly during the first twenty-five years of its existence, was the public outcry against the physical appearance and content of many of the books issued. Early on, Pocket Books experienced censorship attempts when the content and cover of its 1939 edition of John O'Hara's *Appointment in Samarra* met with protest. The publisher quickly took it out of circulation. (See also Plate 8a.) Perhaps paperback publishing's most bizarre instance of self-censorship occurred in Great Britain. Allen Lane, Penguin founder, was "particularly affronted" by a book his company published. With a friend he staged a midnight raid on his own warehouse. After breaking in, he loaded the offending books on a truck and carried them to his farm some miles away, where they were immediately burned.

Throughout the late 1940s and early 1950s paperback books were attacked by censoring agencies, both official and unofficial, that sought to purge the wire racks of lurid literature. This period of lost esteem for Pocket Books and other paperback houses has been described as a time of "sex, sensationalism, and statutory rape." The inquiring and censoring agencies ranged from "public-spirited" groups and organizations with religious affiliations to local and state police. In 1952 the U.S. House of Representatives appointed a Select Committee on Current Pornographic Materials, popularly known as the Gathings Committee, to investigate the editorial selection and marketing practices of magazine and paperback publishers. (See Plate 7b.) The hearings conducted by the committee revealed, if nothing else, the ignorance of certain publishing executives about the content of the books they published.

The hearings also put a damper on some of the more heavy-handed packaging practices of paperback publishers. The dominant style of cover illustration at this time was a brooding

CENSORSHIP

A "sensational" Pocket Books cover, mild by today's standards as well as those of the 1950s. Illustrator unknown.

The protests of the early fifties found publishers zipping up their cover art. TOP: 1951 edition, illustrated by Robert Stanley. ABOVE: 1952 reissue.

realism to which a thick veneer of sex and sadism was imposed. (See Plates 9a–d.) Frequently, however, there was little or nothing inside the book to support promises made by the cover art and copy.

Many books under attack were publications by serious writers. These books often relied on cover sensationalism to attract prospective buyers who had never heard of the author. Publishers often defended this kind of packaging by claiming that the alluring covers attracted a new and broader readership, which otherwise would not have been led to this fine literature. Furthermore, they claimed to do it for the reader's own good. One softcover art director, however, was led to summarize crassly the packaging philosophy practiced by most publishers of the era: "I believe that the only good cover art is one that brings the twenty-five cents across the counter."

Existing on the fringes of mass market publishing for the past forty years have been dozens of publishers of erotic and semi-erotic "adult" (male sophisticate) literature. A few of these companies have a history of rapid, clandestine moves from state to state, and their imprints often parody established paperback publishers: Candid Readers, Boudoir Books, Bedroom Publications, Pigalle Press, Ram Books, Rear Window, and Pain Library Classics.

The late 1940s saw the rise of two other practices that stirred the ire of some paperback readers and resulted in scrutiny by another government investigating unit, the Federal Trade Commission (FTC). Both practices also related to cover design. Heavily criticized as misleading the public was the practice of abridgment without conspicuous notice. Paper was and still is the largest single cost element in book manufacturing. In the postwar 1940s, when paper costs rose sharply and the twenty-five-cent cover price was still the rule, the practice of cutting a longer work became widespread.

Pressure from the FTC forced publishers to note on the front cover the original title (often shown in parentheses) and to state that the book was an abridgment. To counter the then-widespread belief that paperback books were always shortened versions of the original hardcover texts, publishers for many years prominently proclaimed on all uncut titles the fact that the work was identical to the original, "complete and unabridged."

Changing the title for a reprint edition to make it more provocative than the original version and more compatible with sensational cover art was another practice widely used by mass market publishers. Often these title changes were not noted on the new edition, leaving publishers justifiably open to charges of misleading the public. An author is reported to have spotted a book while browsing by a writer with a name identical to his own. After closer examination he discovered that his own tale of newspaper reporting in the hub of the Midwest, *Deadlines and Monkeyshines,* had been retitled *Chicago—City of Sin.*

5
Maturity of an Industry

The history of paperback publishing from the mid-1950s to the present is marked by steady growth and evolution. Initially the industry played a subservient role to that of hardcover publishers. This is exemplified by an incident Victor Weybright told about the observance of George Bernard Shaw's ninetieth birthday, which was planned in 1946 by Shaw's American hardcover publisher, Dodd, Mead. Weybright, who was at the time editor-in-chief of the Penguin branch in New York, related: "When I told Howard Lewis of Dodd, Mead that I thought that we should be in on the celebration, which was to take place at the Waldorf-Astoria, he looked at our paperbound editions of *Saint Joan, Pygmalion* and *Major Barbara* and suggested that we have our own party at the Automat."

In a relatively short time, however, paperback publishers began to shed their lower-class status and their dependence on the goodwill of original hardcover publishers and moved to a position of independence and, eventually, dominance within the book industry. Today the softcover industry's ability to acquire bestselling authors, commission original works, publish and promote media tie-ins, and, in particular, pay large sums for reprint rights have made it the most dynamic and one of the most profitable segments of the contemporary book industry. Numbers underscore this growth, which is commonly called "the paperback revolution." By the end of 1939 an estimated 3 million paperbacks had been sold. By 1946, however, an observer of the paperback publishing scene noted in *Publishers Weekly* that "a million-copy sale is peanuts today." In 1949, ten years after Robert de Graff issued his first ten Pocket Books, total paperback book sales for the year were calculated at 175 million. Three years later, when unit sales exceeded 250 million copies, *Business Week* dubbed paperbound books "the zoom in publishing." Figures for 1979 estimate 535 million paperbacks sold; publisher receipts for these sales were slightly over $600 million.

Attitudes surrounding mass market publishing were also changing at the same time. In 1913 *The Atlantic Monthly* quoted an author as saying, "I should consider myself disgraced if I had written a book which in these days sold one hundred thousand copies." In contrast, forty years later, Edmund Wilson wrote to his literary agent: "I am making money out of my paperback editions . . . and feel a little, for the first time in my life, as if I were a real success. . . ."

Perhaps the first recognition that the relationship between hardcover publishers and the paperback houses was evolving was described in 1951, when *The New York Times* reported that "an increasing number of trade books are being brought out only after reprint rights have been guaranteed." The subsidiary income generated from paperback reprint sales increased in importance and amount through the 1960s, leading to the well-known paperback auctions and million-dollar advances that commanded headline attention in the 1970s.

The ability of paperback publishers to pay sizable advances not only for "blockbuster" reprints but also for less well-known books and even for category titles led to another development. As noted earlier, reprinted authors began to be lured away from their original hardcover publishers, and literary agents started bringing new authors to paperback houses first. Writers, both new and established, frequently estimated that they would make more money dealing first with a softcover house, which would either issue their works in original paperback editions or, retaining reprint rights, place the book with a trade-book publisher for a hardcover edition. Hardcover publishers call this practice of purchasing first publication rights from a paperback publisher "buying backward." Some hardcover publishers retaliated by not renewing reprint contracts for titles that were particularly successful on mass market backlists. Instead, they incorporated the regained titles into their own newly established *trade* paperback series.

By the early 1960s, several mass market publishers responded in kind by establishing their own hardcover trade-book lines. Pocket Books, which always had a close eye on the hardcover output of its stepparent, Simon & Schuster, instituted Trident Press; Dell Books sponsored the Dial hardcover line; NAL at various times has published in hardcover under its own imprint or controlled the hardcover imprint of the now-defunct World Publishing Company. In 1980 even Bantam, which had long resisted hardcover involvement, issued their first cloth edition, Tom Robbins's *Still Life with Woodpecker*. The success of these imprints has been mixed; however, they symbolize the determination of paperback publishers to build their own stable of authors, further blurring the already shaky distinctions between hardcover and paperback publishers.

TRADE PAPERBACKS

Another (and more profitable) response to competition from hardcover publishers was the trade paperback, which by the early 1970s was being published by almost all the major mass market houses.

Trade paperbacks trace their roots back to Penguin Books with even more certainty than mass market publications. During and immediately after World War II, the American branch of the company had enlarged its own semi-independent publishing program, which was principally comprised of Penguin and Pelican imprints. The former series began to evolve into a line of books closely resembling American mass market imprints. The Pelican imprint, however, offered serious nonfiction and classics of world literature similar to the English Pelican series. In 1948, when the New American Library evolved from the American Penguin publishing program, the Pelican imprint changed to Mentor Books. This venerable mass market imprint became the direct forerunner of the American trade paperback by attracting a broad spectrum of readers, especially on campuses, to its reprints of classics of world literature and serious nonfiction.

Penguin Books reentered the American market in 1949, when

a distribution center was opened in Baltimore. As happened in the early 1940s, the new United States branch soon began to publish titles on its own. By 1962 Penguin had opened editorial offices in New York, and in 1975 Penguin England, which had been acquired by a larger company, purchased The Viking Press and incorporated the Viking Compass and Portable paperback imprints into its own softcover series. Throughout its history, both in England and the United States, the Penguin format has resembled that of American mass market publishers; however, Penguin's publishing practices more closely resemble those of U.S. trade paperback publishing in the quality of their list, the conservativeness of their cover designs, and their channels of distribution.

The Anchor series, begun by Doubleday in 1953, is usually cited as the first American *trade* paperback series. In fact, however, almost a dozen other successful paperback imprints not sponsored by mass market houses were being published at this time. Several, including Dover, Rider, and Hafner, continue to issue books today.

But Anchor Books and the trade paperback series that were patterned after it differed from these earlier nonmass market paperback imprints. Most of these newer series were issued by major hardcover houses. They exploited an institutional market that earlier paperback imprints, with the exception of Penguin and Mentor Books, had largely ignored. Jason Epstein, the Doubleday editor who conceived the series, saw the nation's growing college student and faculty populations as prime markets for course-related titles that were either out of print or only available in expensive hardcover editions. The prices of the early Anchor Books were usually just under one dollar. Retailing at an average price of 75 cents, Anchor's first four titles were Stendahl's *The Charterhouse of Parma,* Francis Fergusson's *The Idea of a Theater,* D. H. Lawrence's *Studies in Classic American Literature,* and Joseph Bédier's *The Romance of Tristan and Iseult.* The series had an early and durable bestseller in David Reisman's *The Lonely Crowd.*

Almost immediately other established hardcover houses joined the trade paperback rush, including Alfred A. Knopf's Vintage Books, E. P. Dutton's Everyman Paperbacks, and Viking's Compass Books. Fourteen new paperbound imprints were announced at the start of the 1960s. As the decade of the sixties progressed, few general and university press book publishers failed to sponsor trade paperbacks also, which, depending on the critic who reviewed them, were dubbed "quality," "highbrow," or "egghead" books.

In the early 1960s two experiments, both engineered by Leonard Shatzkin, tried to apply mass merchandising techniques to the sale of trade paperbacks. But both Dolphin Books, another Doubleday trade imprint, and Collier Books, a trade paperback line of the Macmillan Company, failed to measure up to their mass market expectations. Each imprint within a relatively short time produced a glut of unsold copies in retail accounts across the United States. Both survived the surgery that was then performed on their marketing programs and continue today as conventional trade paperback series.

The 1970s saw another kind of trade paperback emerge. Sometimes paperback originals—and generally priced somewhere between mass market and hardcover books—these books in content were less weighty than the earlier "egghead" paperbacks and were aimed at the middle-class buying public which frequented the mushrooming retail bookstores that sprang up in shopping centers and revitalized downtowns across the United States. Designed in a variety of sizes and shapes and often heavily illustrated, they have been called "outsized," "oversized," or "large format" paperbacks. Their popularity and dimensions demanded special face-out display on retail shelves or tables formerly reserved for hardcover books.

Most mass market houses today also publish both types of trade paperbacks, which further blurs distinctions between them and other general book publishers. NAL's Meridian and Dell's Delta are the longest-established *trade* imprints sponsored by mass market publishers.

CORPORATE OWNERSHIP

Beginning in the early 1960s, privately owned softcover publishers became publicly owned corporations on their own initiative, or were acquired by larger corporate organizations. One positive result was the infusion of much-needed capital to cover the ever-escalating advances for hardcovers and the costs of production, sales, and advertising necessary to make these reprints succeed.

Mass market houses' profit margins and growth through the 1960s and 1970s made them attractive acquisitions for large corporations, especially those in the communications industry seeking to further diversify their holdings. Today, every major mass market paperback house is owned by a larger corporation. New American Library was one of the first to give up its independence when it was acquired in 1960 by the Times Mirror Company, a holding company built around the Los Angeles newspaper owned by the Chandler family. Pocket Books became a division of Simon & Schuster in 1966. Ten years later S&S was acquired by Gulf + Western, thus gaining an affiliation with another well-known entertainment company, Paramount Pictures. CBS acquired two paperback houses, Popular Library and Fawcett, in the 1970s. Ballantine Books is part of Random House, which recently was sold by RCA to the Newhouse newspaper chain. Warner Books is owned by Warner Communications, Berkley and Jove Books by MCA, and Ace Books by Filmways. Meanwhile, Dell and Avon are held by "modest-size" publishers with diversified interests, Doubleday and the Hearst Corporation, respectively.

Writers, educators, booksellers, and even some publishers have raised cries of concern over corporate ownership. Some fear that corporations will exert direct control on the editorial selection of their publishing subsidiaries. Yet few specific examples of large parent corporations directly influencing editorial decisions are known, probably because few exist. More valid are concerns about the "bottom-line syndrome." Corporate ownership encourages a publisher to issue that which is most profitable, but not necessarily what is best. This in turn promotes a tendency in American paperback publishing that needs little encouragement: to imitate or duplicate that which already has been successful. Publishers are constantly criticized for concentrating promotion and advertising dollars on blockbuster titles and ignoring the mid-list books, which are left to fend for themselves on the paperback racks.

BOOKSELLERS   Corporate acquisition has also changed the face of retail book-selling in the United States. In the second half of the 1970s, general book publishers, including paperback houses, discovered that their two most important accounts were Walden Book Company (which once specialized in rental libraries) and B. Dalton. Both of these bookstore franchises are owned by large chain department-store companies that have, like their book publishing counterparts, encouraged bullish expansion.

In the 1940s and 1950s, retail bookstores generally did not exist outside of large metropolitan areas and college towns. They were specialty stores, frequently selling only hardcover titles and attracting a minority of the population, the educated upper-middle class. *The New York Times* stated in 1960 that the estimated 1,450 bookstores in the United States had not increased in number in a century.

The 1960s and 1970s saw a dramatic growth of retail bookstores—college stores, wholesaler-owned stores, and especially bookstore chains—and by 1980 they numbered almost fourteen thousand general bookstores. Paperbacks are credited with democratizing the retail bookstore, which today caters to readers who grew up with paperback racks in drugstores, newsstands, and supermarkets and had paperbacks assigned as required reading in school and college classrooms.

THE MEDIA   The advantages to the publisher of a film being made from one of his publications have already been noted. While *Wuthering Heights* was Robert de Graff's earliest bestseller, it is doubtful whether the producers of the successful motion picture saw the Pocket Books edition as much help at the box office. It would be many years before film producers saw the movie tie-in paperback as anything more than a minor method of promoting their films. For paperback publishers, however, these films, often made well after a first paperback edition had appeared, sometimes brought in unexpected and substantial new revenues. New softcover editions (reissues) would be printed, sometimes with cover illustrations radically different in theme from earlier editions—often photographs or illustrations of the film's stars. "Now that you've enjoyed the movie, read the book," publishers urged.

1

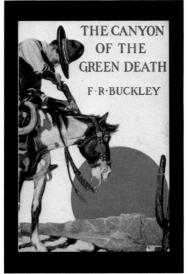

2

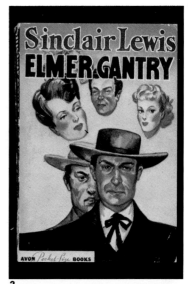

3

4a

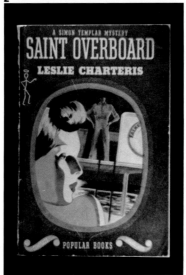

4b

5

1. Beadle's Frontier Series published by Iver & Co. (1908, 4¹³/₁₆'' x 7³/₁₆''). See p.29.

4a. Dell No. 1 (1943). Illustrated by William Strohmer.

2. Published under Doubleday's Garden City Publishing Company imprint, the first paperback series which Robert de Graff directed. Its short-lived competition with Street & Smith publications caused De Graff later to dub it the ''Omelet Library'' (1923, 5'' x 7⁵/₁₆''). See p.31.

4b. Popular Library No. 1 (1943). Illustrated by H. Lawrence Hoffman.

3. The first Avon paperback, published in 1941 (4½'' x 6½''). Illustrator unknown. See p.47.

5. Ace Double edition D-1 (1952). Illustrated by Norman Saunders. See pp.51,122.

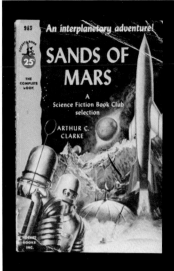

6a

6b

7a

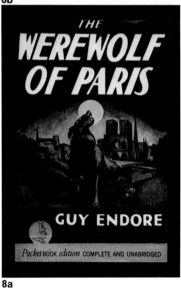

7b

8a

8b

6a, b. Pocket Books silver-backed rocketship covers published in 1954 and illustrated by Robert Schulz.

7a. Popular Library (1949). Illustrated by Earle Bergey.

7b. Fawcett Gold Medal (1950). Illustrated by Baryé Phillips. This title was a prime target in 1952 of the U.S. House of Representatives Select Committee on Current Pornographic Materials. See pp.55,70.

8a. A Pocket Books title (1941), which, like *Appointment in Samarra,* was attacked as too sensational. Illustrator unknown.

8b. An even more sensational cover appeared ten years later when Avon next reprinted it in paperback. Illustrator unknown. See p.55.

9a. Popular Library (1951). Illustrated by Rudolph Belarski. **9b.** Signet (1952). Illustrated by Carl Bobertz. **9c.** Avon (1948). Illustrator unknown. **9d.** Beacon (1954). Illustrator unknown. See p.56.

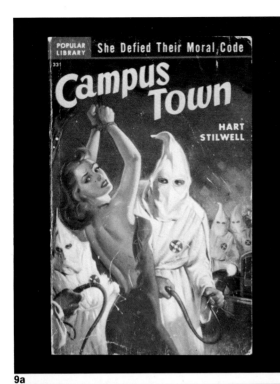

9a

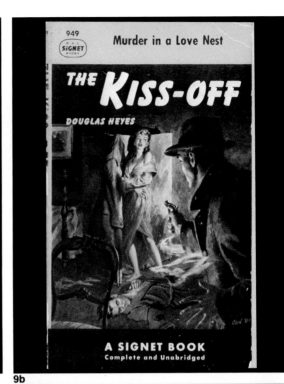

9b

9c

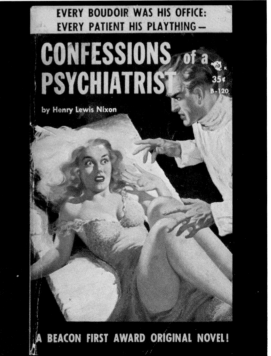

9d

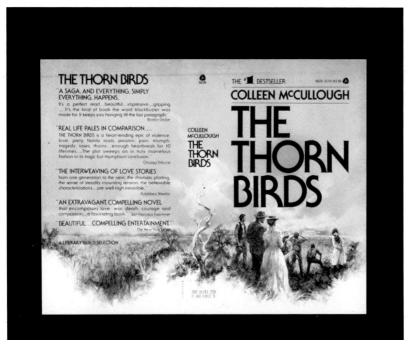

10. "Generation saga and epic of the land," Avon (1978). Illustrated by Tom Hall. See p.81.

10

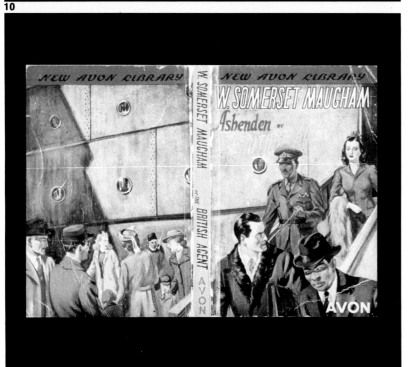

11. The three basic approaches to illustrating a book cover: **11a.** Scene: Avon (1943), an example of an early wraparound cover, a design that became popular in the 1970s. Illustrator unknown.

11a

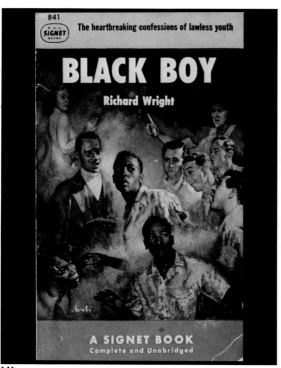

11b

11c

11b. Vignette: Signet (1951). Illustrated by James Avati.
11c. Symbol: Avon (1944). Illustrator unknown. See p.87.

12. Bantam # 786. Illustrated by C. C. Beill. See p.91.

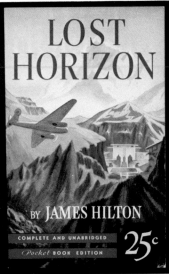

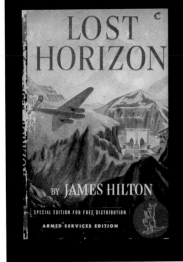

13a

13b

13c

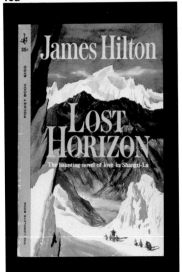

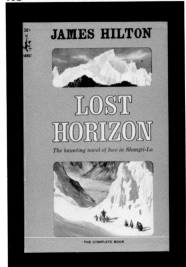

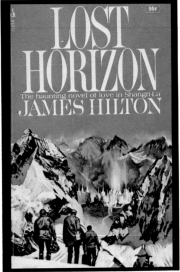

13d

13e

13f

13. Forty years of *Lost Horizon* in a Pocket Books format: **13a.** First printing (1939). Illustrated by Isadore Steinberg.

13d. Forty-seventh printing (1961). Illustrator unknown.

13b. Armed Services Edition (circa 1942).

13e. Sixty-fifth printing (1967). Illustrator unknown.

13c. Forty-fourth printing (1959). Illustrated by Tom Dunn.

13f. Seventy-fourth printing (1972). Illustrator unknown.

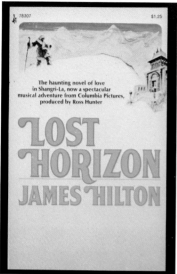

13g

13h

14a

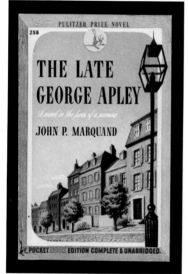

14b

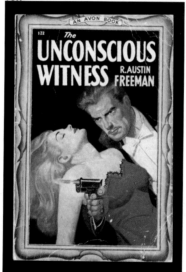

14c

14d

13g. Seventy-ninth printing (1974). Illustrator unknown.

14b. Pocket Books (1944). Illustrated by Leo Manso.

13h. Fortieth anniversary of Pocket Books edition, eightieth printing (1979). Redrawn by Terry McKee. See p.93.

14c. Avon (1947). Illustrator unknown.

14. A popular design feature, the framed cover, has been and will remain a popular method of projecting the contents of a work of fiction.
14a. Log Cabin Press (not dated). Illustrator unknown. 4⁹/₁₆″ x 6⁷/₈″.

14d. Popular Library (1977). Illustrated by James Campbell. See p.101.

15a

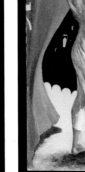

15b

16a

16b

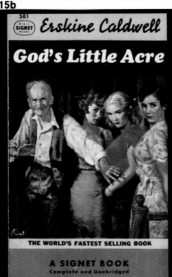

16c

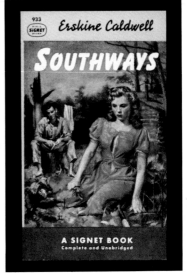

16d

15. The cover art did not harm Pocket Books' sales of this French classic in the 1940s. They were daring covers for a company whose cover art at this time was quite conservative.
15a. 1941. Illustrator unknown.

16b. Bantam (1949).

15b. 1947. Illustrator unknown. See p.100.

16c. Signet (1950).

16. Early James Avati covers:
16a. Signet (1949).

16d. Signet (1952). See p.102.

With the rise of the "blockbuster" bestseller titles of the 1960s, paperback publishers began drawing the direct attention of film (and later television) producers, who began to see paperback success as a box office foundation made up of the millions who had bought the softcover bestseller. "If you liked the book, you're going to love the movie" became a popular slogan of the film industry.

In the 1970s the high-priced reprint auctions hardcover publishers held for paperbacks redoubled this film and television interest. Film or television options were often sold not only before paperback publication but also before the hardcover publication date. Today, when important book properties are being prepared for publication, there is a tendency to orchestrate a comprehensive marketing campaign, tying together hardcover and paperback publication and film and television broadcast well in advance of any production.

As an advertising and promotional tool, radio and television were used extensively in the 1970s to broaden the sales of important titles in a wide range of categories. These often were original paperbacks or reprints of poor-selling hardcover editions that the publisher believed had the makings of a paperback bestseller. Paperback publishers today take particular pride in pointing out million-copy-selling reprints whose original hardcover sale barely covered production costs. They frequently cite carefully planned and expensive media campaigns as their not-too-secret ingredient. These promotion and advertising blitzes have drawn both the envy and imitation of hardcover publishers while encouraging the defection of bestselling writers to softcover houses.

The imaginative and liberal application of promotion, publicity, and advertising is still another element of the paperbound publishers' success.

Ghostly early media tie-in covers. TOP: Pocket Books, fourth printing (1942). ABOVE: Pocket Books (1949).

6
Leading Publishers

Before large sums of money were infused into the paperback industry, a handful of companies accounted for a high percentage of sales. In the 1950s and 1960s Pocket Books saw New American Library, Bantam, Dell, and Fawcett rise to challenge its leadership and acquire their share of mass market paperback sales. While these five companies are still at the top of the heap, subsequent corporate acquisitions and investment have encouraged smaller operations to compete with them. Ballantine, Avon, and the relatively new Warner imprint have in recent years competed on almost equal terms with the big five. At the beginning of the 1980s these eight publishers accounted for as much as 75 percent of domestic paperback sales, although in 1977, according to the U.S. Census Bureau, twenty-one mass market publishers had sales exceeding $100,000.

Out of this group of eight, one paperback house today is recognized as the leader, in much the same way that Pocket Books dominated the industry in the 1940s. Since the mid-1950s Bantam Books has built editorial, production, and marketing departments that are second to none in paperback publishing.

BANTAM BOOKS

Despite severe distribution problems Bantam held on following Ian Ballantine's departure in 1952. Oscar Dystel, a former magazine editor, arrived in June 1954 to take charge of the leaderless publishing house as president, and for the next twenty-five years

Dystel drew around him some of the most talented people in the publishing business. The Bantam editorial department not only acquired rights to solid hardcover bestsellers but also developed both fiction and nonfiction lines that have provided the company with the deepest, most prestigious backlist in the paperback industry. The gallery of distinguished twentieth-century writers who have appeared in paperback under the Bantam imprint includes Ernest Hemingway, John Steinbeck, John O'Hara, Conrad Richter, Robert Penn Warren, John Barth, Philip Roth, E. L. Doctorow, John Knowles, Barbara Tuchman, Carson McCullers, Arthur Miller, Ray Bradbury, Aldous Huxley, Mary Renault, Graham Greene, Winston Churchill, Hermann Hesse, André Schwarz-Bart, and Alexander Solzhenitsyn.

The Bantam bestseller list includes titles that have become symbols of American culture, including *Jaws, Future Shock, Valley of the Dolls, The Chariots of the Gods?, Everything You Always Wanted to Know About Sex But Were Afraid to Ask, The Exorcist, The Guinness Book of World Records, Exodus, Airport, Passages, The Amityville Horror,* and *Princess Daisy.* Bantam also has a stable of popular fiction writers whose works, while strictly limited to a particular category, have had sales reaching well beyond their core of dedicated readers: Ross Macdonald (mysteries), Grace Livingston Hill and Emilie Loring (romances), and Louis L'Amour (Westerns).

Bantam perfected the "instant" book, a publication responding to a current event by appearing on newsstands less than a week after the event. Bantam has published more than seventy "Extras," ranging in subject from the historic visit of Pope Paul VI to the United States in 1965 to the Jonestown massacre in 1978. *Miracle on Ice,* an "instant" account of the United States hockey victories at the 1980 Winter Olympics at Lake Placid, was a finished book forty-six and a quarter hours after the manuscript was completed. Bantam's marketing and promotion departments are especially adept at media tie-ins. Gerald Green's novelization of his script of *Holocaust,* a four-part television drama aired in the spring of 1978, resulted in the distribution of nearly 2 million copies by the end of that year. Hank Searls's novelization of *Jaws 2,* published in conjunction with the 1978 release of the film, was one of that year's top bestsellers, with close to 4 million copies in print. Since the late 1950s Ban-

Leading Publishers

67

tam's cover art and design have been studied and imitated throughout the book industry.

Bantam's success has attracted acquisition by large corporations and holding companies. Since 1968 control of the company has passed through four corporate giants. In 1980 the Bertelsmann Publishing Group of West Germany assumed total ownership of the company.

DELL BOOKS

The fortunes of Dell Books rose dramatically with the publication of the first real blockbuster of the paperback industry, Grace Metalious's *Peyton Place.* The paperback edition found its way to a mass audience of undreamed-of size, which placed it at the top of 1957 bestseller lists, where it stayed through 1958. A hit Hollywood film, and subsequent novel and television sequels and serializations, have maintained the popularity of the *Peyton Place* phenomenon.

In the 1970s Bantam experienced similar blockbuster success with *Jaws* and *The Exorcist,* NAL with *Love Story,* Fawcett with *The Godfather,* Avon with *The Thorn Birds,* and Dell, again, with *Roots.* But in the history of paperback publishing no single book ever matched the power of *Peyton Place,* both to change the fortunes of a publisher and to become a permanent symbol for an American way of life. The success of *Peyton Place* encouraged Dell in the early 1960s to add new wings to its house by taking over the editorial and production functions that Western Publishing had previously been performing for it.

Joining *Peyton Place* on the bestseller lists of the late 1950s were two other Dell titles, Françoise Sagan's *Bonjour Tristesse* and Robert Traver's *Anatomy of a Murder.* In the 1960s, James Baldwin's *Another Country* and Joseph Heller's *Catch-22* were distinguished Dell reprints. Recently, the police novels of Joseph Wambaugh have joined *The Other Side of Midnight* by Sidney Sheldon and *Rosemary's Baby* by Ira Levin on Dell's all-time bestseller list. Success also was achieved in the late 1970s with the television tie-ins of *Roots* and *Rich Man, Poor Man,* as well as the fiction of Belva Plain, Howard Fast, and Danielle Steel.

Dell's Laurel Leaf Library for young adults and Yearling Books for pre-teens comprise the strongest children's book list in paperback publishing.

Dial and Delacorte, Dell Publishing imprints since the early 1960s, have become by far the most successful hardcover lines sponsored by mass market publishers. In 1924, at age sixteen, Helen Meyer joined Dell when it was a pulp magazine publisher. Meyer has guided Dell's book ventures since their beginning in 1942 and has become the most respected woman executive in contemporary U.S. publishing. She was named president of the company in 1957, a title she retained until shortly after Dell's acquisition by Doubleday in 1976.

Bantam's list of recognized twentieth-century writers is rivaled only by the distinguished authors New American Library has published over the last thirty years, including William Faulkner, George Orwell, D. H. Lawrence, Edith Hamilton, Boris Pasternak, James Jones, Truman Capote, Mary McCarthy, James Baldwin, Rachel Carson, James T. Farrell, E. L. Doctorow, Jack Kerouac, Ayn Rand, Ken Kesey, J. D. Salinger, John Fowles, Earl Thompson, Anne Fremantle, John Kenneth Galbraith, Shirley Ann Grau, Margaret Mead, Joseph Lash, Robert Heinlein, Arthur Koestler, Sinclair Lewis, Alberto Moravia, Flannery O'Connor, Georges Simenon, C. P. Snow, William Styron, and Gore Vidal. NAL's distinguished Mentor imprint continues to compete for classroom adoption with the trade paperback imprints it encouraged to start in the 1950s, as does its line of classic reprints, Signet Classics.

NEW AMERICAN LIBRARY

In the late 1950s NAL began publishing the suspense fiction of Ian Fleming. Perhaps the most successful author series in publishing, James Bond's exotic adventures are dead-certain sales successes into which fresh promotional adrenaline is pumped whenever a new film based on one of the novels opens.

NAL has seldom been reluctant to enter into the bidding for reprint rights. It is credited with being the first company to pay a substantial reprint advance. In 1949 it bought Norman Mailer's *The Naked and the Dead* for $35,000, and followed in 1954 with $100,000 for James Jones's *From Here to Eternity*. However, less than a decade later, NAL's editor-in-chief, Victor Weybright, who made these first purchases, lamented that "the cruelest and most savage competition [in the paperback publishing industry] is in the editorial field which forces publishers to bid against each other to reprint the big, popular titles that can be sold by the millions." In 1973, NAL paid the then record-breaking advance for a nonfiction title of $1.5 million—for reprint rights to *The Joy of Cooking*. In 1978 it broke existing fiction records when it spent $2.2 million for Mario Puzo's *Fools Die* and the right to reissue *The Godfather*.

After a decline in the late 1960s and early 1970s, NAL's fortunes rose with publication in 1975 of Erich Segal's *Love Story*. One of fiction's all-time bestsellers, it was followed in the second half of the 1970s by the soaring successes of *Fear of Flying* by Erica Jong and *Coma* by Robin Cook. Horror tales have also contributed to NAL's resurgence, especially those by Stephen King *(Carrie, Salem's Lot, The Shining, Night Shift)*.

The convolutions of management which the publishing company experienced during its first decade under the ownership of the Times Mirror Company are frequently cited as examples of the evils that can occur when a sensitively managed book publishing operation is acquired by a large impersonal corporation.

FAWCETT

FAWCETT

Throughout its history Fawcett has maintained its reputation as a successful publisher of original fiction. The earliest bestseller of its Gold Medal imprint was Tereska Torres, *Women's Barracks* (see Plate 7b), whose sales undoubtedly were not harmed by its being a prominent exhibit of the Gathings Committee during the 1952 congressional probe of obscene magazines and paperbacks. In 1958 Fawcett added a new twist to the popular Southern fiction of Erskine Caldwell and John Faulkner when it published Kyle Onstott's titillating novel of miscegenation in the antebellum South, *Mandingo*. This started a wave of "plantation" literature in the 1960s and early 1970s and laid the groundwork for the historical romance originals of the latter 1970s. Fawcett has always published extensively in category literature, particularly romance and suspense.

Fawcett acquired its reputation as an aggressive bidder for hardcover bestsellers in 1955, when it paid a record-setting $101,505 advance for *By Love Possessed* by James Gould Cozzens. Fresh from introducing its new Crest imprint, this was Fawcett's way, as it has been for every paperback publisher since then, of announcing that it was around. Softcover houses have been accused of knowingly paying more money for reprint rights than sales projections for that title alone would warrant. Such books, well known and in a certain way prestigious, are seen as "loss leaders," which draw the attention of wholesale and retail book- and chain-store buyers and thus increase orders for all new books on the publisher's list.

Over the next twenty-five years, Fawcett continued to buy the big book, often setting new records for advances for a particular kind of literature. Among the titles for which they have successfully bid are *The Rise and Fall of the Third Reich* by William Shirer, *The Godfather* by Mario Puzo, and several recent works by James Michener. In 1978 a new nonfiction plateau for advances was reached when $2.25 million was paid for *Linda Goodman's Love Signs*. Among the more recent bestselling authors on the Fawcett list are John Updike, Erma Bombeck, and John D. MacDonald, who in 1950 had published his first original paperback, *The Brass Cupcake,* in the Gold Medal series. In January 1977 Fawcett was purchased by CBS, which six years earlier had acquired another mass market imprint, Popular Library.

POPULAR LIBRARY

Since its inception in 1942 the Popular Library conifer logo has survived a series of acquisitions and transplants. The last occurred in the late 1970s, when it became an imprint of Fawcett. Before this last move Popular Library had been an independent mass market publishing subsidiary of CBS, along with the now-defunct Curtis Book imprint. In the summer of 1981 CBS reluctantly agreed to sell its Popular Library imprint, terminating litigation begun in 1978 by the U.S. Department of Justice. The government had charged that the merger of the Fawcett and Popular Library imprints seriously diminished competition in the paperback industry.

Outstanding among Popular Library's publications have been *Webster's New World Dictionary,* one of the top five all-time paperback bestsellers, and Harper Lee's poignant *To Kill a Mockingbird.* In the 1950s Polly Adler's *A House Is Not a Home* and Lillian Roth's *I'll Cry Tomorrow,* as well as *Seize the Day* and *The Adventures of Augie March* by Saul Bellow, were notable Popular Library publications.

POCKET BOOKS

Until recently, and in contrast with most of the other major paperback publishers, Pocket Books pointedly did not engage in the hot scrambling that surrounded the auctions and acquisitions of bestselling paperback books in the 1960s and 1970s. Instead, over much of the last thirty years the company has developed and relied on its solid backlist, its proximity to Simon & Schuster, and a good category publishing program to maintain steady if not always headline-making sales.

When the company celebrated its fortieth anniversary in 1979, it could cite two nonfiction titles as all-time bestsellers: Dr. Spock's *Baby and Child Care,* first published in 1946, and *The Merriam-Webster Pocket Dictionary,* which first appeared in 1947. Several other language and reference works of long standing on the Pocket list continue to sell tens of thousands each year, as do the nonfiction classics *Anne Frank: The Diary of a Young Girl* and John F. Kennedy's *Profiles in Courage.*

For the past twenty years the star writer on Pocket Books' list has been Harold Robbins; few twentieth-century writers can match his softcover sales. In fiction, the prolific pens of whodunit writers Erle Stanley Gardner and Agatha Christie have resulted in gratifying sales for Pocket, along with the Westerns of Zane Grey and Max Brand.

In 1944 Marshall Field III, the Chicago newspaper magnate, made the first corporate acquisition of a contemporary mass market publisher when he acquired Pocket Books for $3 million, a sum now paid for reprint rights in a hardline reprint auction. Leon Shimkin, who had aided Robert de Graff as the company's first treasurer, became co-owner in 1957, when he and a partner bought Pocket Books from the Field estate. In 1966 it was merged with Simon & Schuster, which Shimkin also controlled. In 1975 Shimkin sold S&S, together with the Pocket Books imprint, to Gulf + Western.

The close of the 1970s saw Pocket Books projecting a fresh image as an aggressive promoter of bestselling fiction by authors such as Herman Wouk, Richard Brautigan, Bernard Malamud, Morris West, Joan Didion, V. C. Andrews, Judith Rossner, and John Irving, in addition to Robbins, and setting what was then a record for an unpublished first novel by advancing the princely sum of $285,000 to author Steve Krantz (husband of Judith Krantz of *Scruples* fame) for *Laurel Canyon.*

Avon's growth in the last twenty years was spearheaded by a succession of three very able editors-in-chief, Frank E. Taylor, Peter Mayer, and Walter Meade. Beginning in the early 1960s Avon radically changed the quality and scope of its publishing program, and it entered the 1980s as one of the half dozen largest mass market houses and one of the three most profitable.

Avon's concern for neglected American fiction led to the paperback publication in 1964 of *Call It Sleep*. Originally published in hardcover in 1934, Henry Roth's novel received wide critical acclaim in its reincarnation and became the first paperback to receive front-page coverage in *The New York Times Book Review*. It has been a steady seller for Avon ever since.

In 1972 Avon announced that its entire list for September would be made up of original publications and projected that the following year 40 percent of its list would be originals. A seemingly radical editorial approach at that time, this policy paved the way for the acquisition and original publication of historical romances by Rosemary Rogers and Kathleen Woodiwiss. In the latter half of the 1970s this newly discovered category of women's romantic fiction did not settle into the middle range of sales in which other category literature like Westerns and mysteries found themselves. Instead, Avon and all the other mass market houses who followed suit discovered that sales of historical romances equaled or surpassed reprint editions of hardcover bestsellers for which large advances had been paid.

Among the bestselling Avon titles of the last twenty years are Margery Williams's children's classic *The Velveteen Rabbit,* Richard Bach's *Jonathan Livingston Seagull,* Bel Kaufman's *Up the Down Staircase,* Catherine Marshall's *Christy,* Robin Moore's *The Green Berets,* and, more recently, Colleen McCullough's *The Thorn Birds.* The self-help volumes of Wayne Dyer and Thomas Harris, plus *The Final Days,* Woodward and Bernstein's second Watergate volume, have been nonfiction successes for the company.

From its beginning in 1952 until its acquisition from Intext by Random House in 1973, Ballantine Books was the maverick of the paperback industry. During this period the company, under the leadership of the energetic Ian and Betty Ballantine, became known and respected, particularly among booksellers, for its innovations and its ability to identify or start new reading trends. The single most successful title in the company's history, J. R. R. Tolkien's *The Hobbit,* started a publishing trend toward fantasy literature in 1966, which has since captured millions of readers. In the latter half of the 1960s Ballantine made a much more important contribution to consciousness-raising by supporting the growing concern about world population and ecology with books by movement leaders Paul Ehrlich and the Sierra Club, among others.

Following the Random House acquisition, the publishing program was expanded, and the range of its list began to compete directly with larger mass market houses. Its success with movie tie-in titles, such as *Rocky* and *Star Wars,* in the late 1970s underscored its new competitive position. At the beginning of the 1980s, with writers like Barbara Tuchman, Carl Sagan, John Cheever, and John Gardner, Ballantine ranked among the eight largest mass market publishers.

Shortly after the Random House acquisition, the Ballantines left the company that bore their name and, under the sponsorship of Bantam Books, started a trade paperback publishing company, Peacock Press. By the turn of the decade their editorial leadership at Ballantine had been assumed by another husband-wife combination, Lester and Judy-Lynn Del Rey. In 1981 Ian Ballantine returned to the company as a special consultant.

ACE

Despite being a division of Charter Communications, which is part of Grosset & Dunlap, which in turn is a subsidiary of the parent corporation Filmways, Ace Books has remained essentially a publisher of category fiction, seldom capturing headlines with the payment of large reprint advances or multimillion-copy sales. As it has done since it was founded by A. A. Wyn in 1952, Ace continues to publish Westerns and award-winning science fiction by authors such as Ursula Le Guin, Frank Herbert, and Robert E. Howard. In 1960 Ace pioneered the publication of the first modern gothic novel, *Thunder Heights* by Phyllis A. Whitney. Since then it has sold millions of gothics, a genre that in the

1970s lost readers to the sweeter Harlequins and period romances, as well as the sexier historical romances championed by Avon.

With similar publishing histories and programs, Berkley and Jove have recently been housed together under yet another conglomerate holding company, MCA. Berkley began publishing books in 1955, when the pocket-sized magazines *Chic* and *News,* on which the company was founded, folded. Today Berkley is best known for its fine science fiction and fantasy line, which it greatly expanded in 1964. The following year Berkley was purchased by hardcover trade publisher G. P. Putnam's, which in turn was bought in 1975 by MCA.

Begun in 1949, Pyramid, the forerunner of Jove, experienced several changes in ownership before it was purchased in 1974 by Harcourt Brace Jovanovich. Despite a name change to Jove in 1977, the imprint never achieved the Olympian heights envisioned by HBJ chairman William Jovanovich when he acquired the mass market house. In early 1979 Jove was sold to the MCA-Putnam group.

Entering the 1980s, Berkley and Jove operate independently, even to the point of having different national distributors. Throughout their respective histories both Berkley and Jove-Pyramid have been basically publishers of category fiction. Until recently it was rare for either to compete with larger publishing houses for reprint rights to bestselling or potential bestselling hardcover titles.

The Jove imprint, however, does include one series that has greatly influenced mass market trends and has sold many millions of copies. Just before its acquisition by Harcourt, Pyramid published the first volumes in John Jakes's bicentennial series, the fictional Kent family chronicles. Not only were the first books in this eight-volume saga the single most successful bicentennial-related book venture, each new volume in the series has continued to be a paperback bestseller and to regenerate sales for earlier volumes.

The unparalleled success of this original paperback series also has highlighted the greater role book packagers are playing in paperback publishing. Editorial packagers are people who, among other things, conceive a book or series of books, sell the idea to a publisher, and then line up one or more authors and direct their writing, much the way an actor is directed in a motion-picture performance. Lyle Kenyon Engel, founder in 1949 of the short-lived mass market publishing house Checkerbooks, is perhaps the best-known book packager. Engel, who once remarked, "My head is like a faucet. Every time I turn it on, out pour ideas," helped plan the John Jakes series and has since been involved with packaging similar historical fiction series for most of the major mass market houses.

WARNER BOOKS

Warner Books evolved from Paperback Library after the latter's 1973 acquisition by a corporation that later became Warner Communications, Inc. Warner Books grew steadily in the 1970s, using the business practices that had made its older competitors successful: a full line of book categories, heavy use of promotion and advertising, and aggressive bidding for bestselling works. Warner successes include Woodward and Bernstein's *All the President's Men, Xaviera* by Xaviera Hollander, *Scruples* by Judith Krantz, *Bloodline* and *A Stranger in the Mirror* by Sidney Sheldon, *Audrey Rose* by Frank De Felitta, *Sybil* by Flora Rheta Schreiber, and romantic novels by Phyllis A. Whitney, Dorothy Daniels, and Jennifer Wilde.

HARLEQUIN BOOKS

Harlequin Books, a Canadian-based firm, started publishing a well-rounded line of category fiction in 1949, but by 1964 it published only romances. Not until the early 1970s, however, when W. Lawrence Heisey arrived from Procter & Gamble, did the company begin to make significant inroads into U.S. paperback readership. Heisey, who "did for paperbacks what L'eggs did for pantyhose," stressed his imprint or brand name over book authorship. At the retail level, the books were segregated on their own racks with cover art designed not so much to distinguish one book from another as to convey the similarities among the various stories. All contained the same standard girl-meets-boy formula. Comic books without pictures, their cover prices were usually lower than other newsstand softcover titles. For some readers the books became addictive.

At the end of the 1970s Harlequin was the fastest-growing paperback publisher, with a profit margin greater than any of its U.S. counterparts. At this time the company also began to diversify its list by adding two new fiction imprints: Mystique (gothics) and Raven House (mysteries). Perhaps the surest tribute to Harlequin's success are the romance series which at least four other established paperback houses began in the 1970s in imitation of Harlequin. Contrary to usual American-Canadian business patterns, in 1979 Harlequin was about to acquire a smaller American mass market paperback house, Pinnacle, until it was discouraged from doing so by the U.S. Department of Justice.

PART II
Cover Art and Design

17a

17b

17c

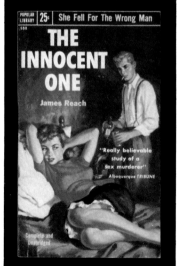

17d

18a

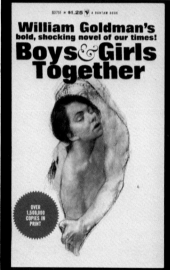

18b

17. A sampling of early 1950s covers (all illustrators unknown):
17a. Popular Library (1953).

17d. Popular Library (1953). See p.103.

17b. Pyramid (1952).

18. Notable Bantam ''white'' covers:
18a. 1964. Illustrated by William Edwards.

17c. Avon (1952).

18b. 1967. Illustrated by James Bama. See p.106.

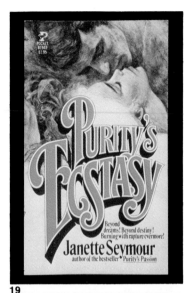

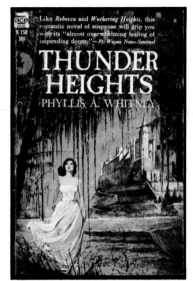

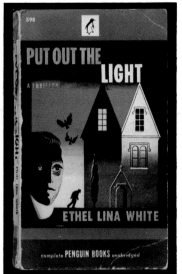

19

20a

20b

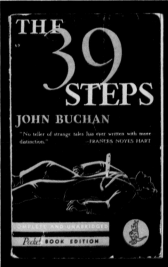

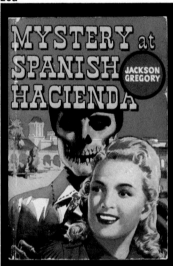

21a

21b

21c

19. An example of a strong logotype fitted into the illustration of veteran cover artist Harry Bennett (Pocket Books, 1978). Its composition and lettering are derivatives of Avon's historical romance designs.

21. Early mystery covers: **21a.** Pocket Books (1940). Illustrator unknown.

20a. Lou Marchetti is generally recognized as having drawn the first "gothic" cover for *Thunder Heights* (Ace, 1960).

21b. Avon (1942). Illustrator unknown.

20b. However, several of the symbols that became part of the gothic formula, including the required "light in the window," were part of Robert Jonas's illustration for *Put Out the Light* (Penguin, 1946). See p.108.

21c. Avon (1949). Illustrator unknown.

21d. Popular Library (1950). Illustrated by Rudolph Belarski. **21e.** Signet (1951). Illustrated by Lou Kimmel. ▶
22. A pair of pulp Western portraits by Norman Saunders: **22a.** Ace (1953). **22b.** Popular Library (1949).

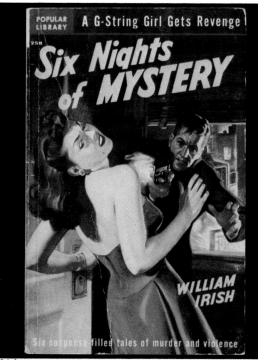

21d

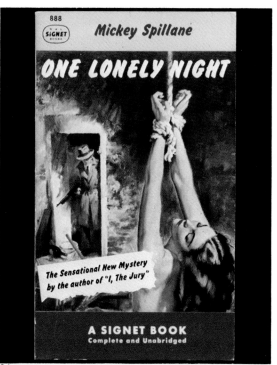

21e

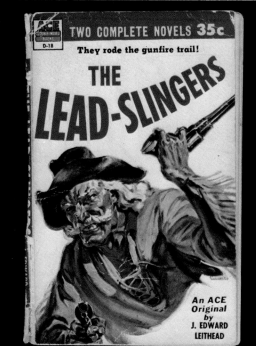

22a

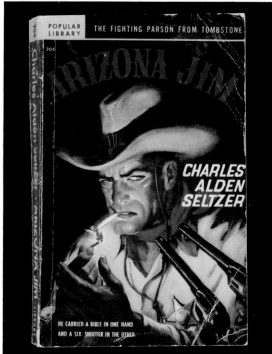

22b

23a

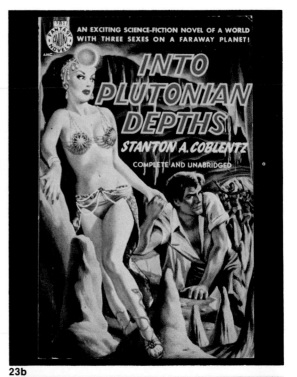

23b

23a, b, c, d. Four fantasy/science fiction covers, all published by Avon in 1950 (illustrators unknown). See p.109.

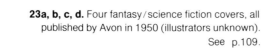

23c

23d

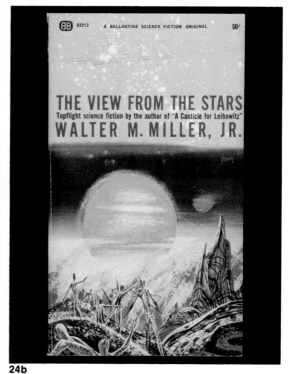

24. Representative science fiction illustrations by Richard Powers: **24a.** Ballantine (1965).
24b. Ballantine (1967). See p.109.

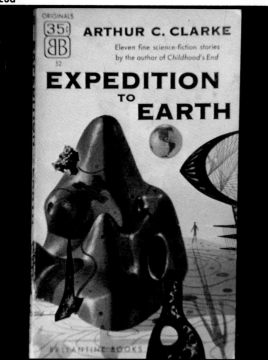

24a

24b

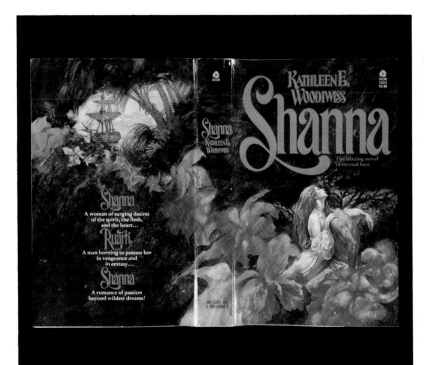

25a

25. Interesting similarities between two front and back covers with tropical settings painted thirty years apart:
25a. Avon (1977, trade paperback edition). Illustrated by Tom Hall. 5⅛″ x 8″.

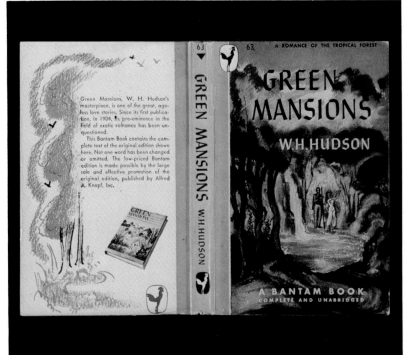

25b

25b. Bantam (1946). Illustrator unknown. See p.110.

26. Two of Milton Glaser's covers for New American Library's Shakespeare series: ▶
26a. 1963.
26b. 1964. See p.112.

27a, b. Covers for two Hermann Hesse titles, illustrated by William Edwards and published by Bantam in the early 1970s. See p.112.

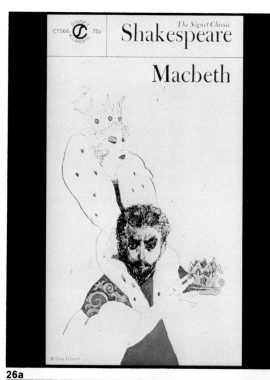

26a

26b

27a

27b

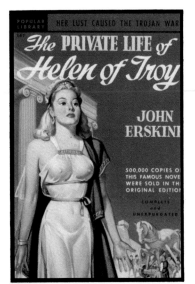

28a

28b

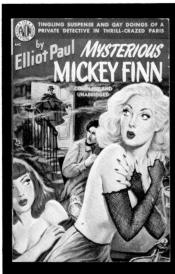

28c

28d

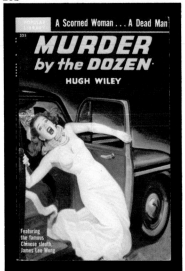

28e

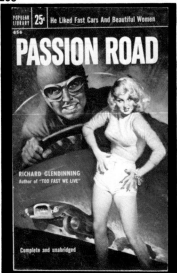

28f

28a. Popular Library (1948). Illustrated by Earle Bergey.

28d. Popular Library (1951). Illustrated by George Rozen.

28b. Avon (1949). Illustrator unknown.

28e. Popular Library (1951). Probably illustrated by S. Cherry.

28c. Avon (1950). Illustrator unknown.

28f. Popular Library (1955). Illustrator unknown. See p.122.

7
The Art Director

In 1977 Avon paid $1.9 million to Harper & Row for reprint
rights to Colleen McCullough's novel *The Thorn Birds*. Avon's
editor-in-chief, Walter Meade, believed that the most crucial
task to face the paperback reprint was the design and selection
of a cover that would convey the book's appeal—and not alienate
any group of readers. Meade reported in *Publishers Weekly* that
in the market testing of possible covers preceding nationwide
publication, Avon found:

> Consumers rejected a version that focused on the book's
> romantic couple (it cut out the men: looked too much like
> a historical romance), and a rendition of the hardcover
> jacket (too cold and literary in the smaller paperback size).
> The majority favored a cover with the Cleary family and
> their land under the big sky (it conveyed the ideas of a
> generation saga and epic of the land). [See Plate 10.]

Paperback cover preparation is an attempt to combine certain
concepts that, on the surface, appear to be mutually exclusive:
the book as a cultural object, with its long-standing tradition as
a permanent record of a writer's thoughts and aspirations, and
the reality of the marketplace, a faceless and seemingly fickle
mass of purchasers whose tastes in reading continually shift. The
interplay of the durability and permanence of the book with the

publisher's conceptions of the marketplace is the essential dynamic of the paperback cover design.

The cover design usually includes title, author's name, editorial and promotion copy, book price and number, publisher's name and logo, and, frequently most important, an illustration. Most of the time this illustration is a painting commissioned from a freelance commercial artist. All other elements of the paperback cover design are adapted to this artwork.

Publishing company officers and department heads, whether involved with editing, production, or marketing, all have an opportunity to influence the cover design. In many houses, cover conferences—group discussions at which a consensus on the right cover is sought—are scheduled regularly. Depending on the size of the publishing company and the importance of a book, anywhere from two or three to several dozen people may have direct or indirect involvement with the creation of a paperback cover.

At the center of all the give-and-take is the publisher's art director. Often an executive of the company, the art director may once have been a cover artist and may occasionally be the one to conceive, lay out, and draw the cover design. In smaller publishing houses art direction may be a one-person operation; however, in major mass market houses a staff of a half dozen or more people generate ideas and help work out design problems.

Today's poster styles of cover design employ the graphic principles of poster design and require careful planning by the art director. After initial input from the book's editor (and often other departments), the art director commonly specifies a basic design approach—symbolic, narrative, or typographic, usually—and suggests the needed signals, i.e., visual clichés that readers of the particular category of literature consciously and unconsciously expect. All design features must be laid out with colors and an integrated pattern whose rhythm captures the attention of the reader.

An art director always has a mixed bag of approaches to select from when working out a cover design for a new or a reissued paperback. This task was summarized philosophically by George Salter, teacher, designer, and illustrator of hundreds of digest-size paperbacks for publisher Lawrence E. Spivak: "We want people to read. I think that we should want that more and more. It seems absolutely imperative to me that the designer, in good faith, make every attempt to let the author say what he has to say and to use his, the designer's, skill to supply the 'how' in the author's mood." (See page 34 for an example of Salter's work.)

In planning a cover the art director sometimes chooses to adapt the hardcover jacket design. With a blockbuster or lead title of interest to movie and television people as well as booksellers, working out a unified promotion and advertising campaign in cooperation with other media is sometimes required. Such a campaign often results in the hardcover dust jacket, the movie poster, television advertising, and the paperback cover all exhibiting the same design.

Art directors may choose to do a straight typographic cover when the author's name or the title of the book itself is well known or particularly striking. If they choose to illustrate the cover, they may select a photograph, as in the case of books by well-known or interesting-looking authors and movie and television tie-in books. Most common, however, are cover designs built around painted illustrations executed by cover artists commissioned by the art director. Painted illustrations are generally realistic representations of people, places, and things, influenced by other commercial media but drawn in the soft-edged style that has dominated cover painting for the last twenty years. Abstract art is not unknown to paperback covers, but it is generally limited to very specialized and appropriate subjects.

The art department staff begins the design of a cover at least a half year in advance of publication. Art directors initiate the process by selecting those elements in the book that:

- best represent the content;
- best project the author's intention in writing the book;
- reflect the publisher's reasons for accepting the book;
- graphically are most compelling;
- connect the material with other successful books or book series;
- reflect the genre or category of the book;
- identify the book as a product of the publisher.

The cover should be relatively easy for a printer to reproduce and for the binder to bind, and it should be reasonably inexpensive to produce. The design must have a contemporary look about it and be fresh and original. But, more important than anything else, the design should stand out on a book rack; it should compel the browser or the shopper to stop and select it from the dozens of others that are on display.

Perhaps Sol Immerman, art director at Pocket Books for almost thirty years, summarized the task best: "Each book [by means of its cover] must be its own salesman, advertisement, and direct contact with the buying public. Of course the basic principles of good selling must govern our thinking. These are (1) attract attention; (2) create interest; and (3) stimulate the desire to purchase." If art directors had only themselves to please, their jobs, although taxing, would not seem overwhelming. However, seldom do they have sole input or final authority over what a cover design contains.

Depending on the size of the publisher and its management practices, the art director presents one or more concepts for each cover to various department heads and executives within the company, individually or in group meetings. The timing and amount of consultation depends on the importance of the acquisition and the difficulty of presenting the book's subject matter in graphic and illustrative form. Genre books such as Westerns or period romances, for example, may require little more than routine consultation before publication. In contrast, blockbuster titles may inspire everyone from the chairman of the board to the stock clerk to supply suggestions.

The editorial staff usually exerts the strongest initial influence on the cover design. Editorial has concerns about the cover that are similar to the author's, particularly a desire for an accurate reflection of the book's content. Besides being closest to the creator and the manuscript, editorial has strong influence because that department is often responsible for supplying the descriptive and promotional copy placed around the cover art. The copy and the illustration cannot appear to make different claims for the same text. The editorial department may also supply a final title for the book or even a pen name for the author.

Another strong influence on the cover art is the production department's concern for the actual costs of reproduction. A standard four-color cover layout is a basic expense, a precalculated portion of a paperback's manufacturing cost. The 1970s saw the arrival of special finishes and gimmick covers that resemble greeting cards and that can increase the cost of cover manufacture and binding two to five times and significantly add to the cost of making the whole book. The book's content and projected sales, however, may not permit the retail price to be raised high enough to allow for this increased cost. Critics of the gimmicky wrappers are not at all sure that this limitation on cover design is such a bad thing.

The heaviest final influence on the art director and design decisions generally springs from the marketing division—sales, promotion, and advertising. Sales managers reflect the preferences of their field force, who in turn claim to know what their buyers like. These wholesale and retail book buyers in turn have their own criteria for what attracts customers at the point of sale.

The stake of the marketing arm of publishers in cover selection cannot be underestimated. Paperback titles generally are sold in quantity to wholesale and retail buyers three or more months in advance of publication, and a crucial tool for publishers' representatives in convincing buyers to place sizable orders are proofs of the books' covers.

The publisher's advertising and promotion personnel, like its sales force in the field, also use cover designs as a tool to generate sales. The cover designs are used in catalogs and order forms and for prepublication trade advertising. Designs are adapted for radio, television, newspaper, mass- and specialty-magazine advertising. Posters may be created from them as well. A variety of point-of-sale display prepacks, display packages holding anywhere from a half dozen to fifty or more copies of the title, are designed for display in prominent spots at retail outlets. They may be freestanding dump bins or counter displays. Elements from the cover design, particularly the cover art, are used to attract customer attention to these foldout display units.

When designing a book cover, art directors keep in mind that the marketing people will be looking for elements in the design that were part of a successful paperback package of the past. Designs cannot be directly imitative, but they are expected to remind all potential buyers in overt and subtle ways of the book's similarity to one or more profit-making titles of the past. The cover design is often the most obvious and contrived manifestation of paperback publishing's penchant to repeat what already has been successful. This was true of the knothole covers of the 1940s, the realistic covers of the 1950s, and the white covers of the 1960s, as well as the gimmicky covers of the 1970s.

Authors sometimes offer cover suggestions or provide photos for use or inspiration and, through their contract with the publisher, or their prestige, may have veto power over the cover art. However, unless it is absolutely necessary, a publisher rarely solicits an author's ideas for a cover illustration. Writers, because they are so close to the work they conceive, develop strong feelings—often difficult to put into concrete terms—about what their book should look like. While they are genuinely concerned with the sales success of their book, they are anxious that the cover not misrepresent intent and content or offend their image of what a volume bearing their name should look like. Publishers believe that most writers lack the objectivity necessary to select cover designs that appeal to the general public.

To survive in this slick jungle of often conflicting perspectives and opinions is no easy task. One art director facetiously defended his work by stating, "If a book sells, it's because the cover works. If it doesn't sell, it's because it's a lousy book."

8
The Cover Artist

At some point during the development of an illustrated cover design a freelance artist is called in to create the illustrative elements. An art director selects a particular cover artist to illustrate a certain book or series of books for a variety of reasons, not the least of which may be personality. For example, the artist and the art director may get along well and may be able to communicate easily with each other. When an art director is dissatisfied with the illustrative and design ideas generated by in-house staff, a good working relationship with a cover artist frequently leads to solutions for problems such as selecting a theme and determining what objects to illustrate, what style of illustration to use, the placement of figures and graphics, and the dominant colors and symbols to use.

When choosing a theme for an illustrated cover, three general approaches are possible: a particular scene in the book may be shown; several different episodes in the book may be incorporated into a series of vignettes; or a symbol representing the book as a whole may be selected. (See Plates 11a–c.) The single-scene approach is used most frequently for genre fiction, which appeals to a fairly well-defined audience of predictable size. The vignette approach, which can show several different situations and scenes running from the front cover around the spine to the back cover, may employ several different illustrative clichés and can appeal to two or more different readership categories. The symbol is an attempt to represent the book as a whole through one image—frequently a small spot illustration centered on the front cover—carefully integrated with editorial and promotion copy.

A single dramatic symbol on a paperback cover has the potential of reaching the widest possible audience because of its relative freedom from explicit content. It can graphically compel the attention of several genre audiences without identifying with any particular one. Symbolic cover illustrations can also take on meanings independent of the book for which they were created— witness the sensation created by the shark symbol of *Jaws* in the mid-1970s.

Many cover artists become known for a particular style, which in turn is often associated with a category of fiction such as Westerns, gothics, historical fiction, or romance. Some can effectively portray moods, backgrounds, children, or women. One artist is known for the skillful way he can draw women's legs. Science fiction illustrators are almost a breed unto themselves, as this genre requires a good knowledge of science and technology, a fantastic imagination, a love for the genre, and a realistic illustrative style—a combination of talents possessed by relatively few successful commercial artists.

Almost all paperback artists have realistic (as opposed to abstract) drawing styles. "The artists who get bought are those who can draw" is a commonplace belief shared by both artist and art director. Relatively little mass market paperback artwork has been influenced by major trends in modern painting. Rather, the realistic representation of a scene or major figure from a piece of fiction has been and still is the core of paperback illustration and reflects the influences of Howard Pyle, Norman Rockwell, and the Wyeths, among other masters of realistic painting and illustration. However, paperback cover artists, as realistic as their art may appear, do not try to capture the world as it actually is. (A photograph can do that.) Instead, they try to create a world that is *just real enough*. The cover illustration must present an image that the prospective buyer is familiar with, one that is real to the imagination. It must be compatible with other escape images presented in movies, television, magazines, and on other books, yet it must have a flair or originality of its own. But this flair cannot be so innovative that it is not easily recognized and interpreted by the prospective buyer. Illustrator-historian Henry Pitz concludes: "The illustrator's picture is not always a delineation of how things actually looked or how they might have looked— *but how a mass audience expected things to look.*"

Different categories of fiction require varying degrees of realism. The male reader of a Western story, publishers believe, wants to smell the gunpowder and taste the dust of the horse-trodden trail. As a result, Western illustration, with its basic primary colors, tends to be very detailed, sometimes photorealistic. At the other extreme, the cover of a nurse romance has none of the West's harsh realism or, for that matter, none of the realism of the waiting room or hospital. Its dreamy pastel colors and pop-art figures promise a misty love affair and a happy ending, a world removed from the routine experiences of the average female reader but still imaginatively attainable.

Until the recent introduction of mechanical gimmickry such as foil, die cuts, embossing, and the like, innovations in paperback cover design usually centered on the cover artist's painting. Artists who come up with a successful new approach or style or perspective ("success" is generally measured by the book's sale) find that they serve as inspiration for large numbers of fellow illustrators.

Cover artists must possess great patience and artistic flexibility. The most durable of them have mastered several realistic styles evolved and perfected over time. Veteran illustrators also know how similar books were treated in the past; they are generally imitators rather than innovators and are frequently asked to adapt some or all of the elements of a competitor's successful cover illustration to a new title or series of books. They must also have some understanding of the publisher's expectations, the pressures on the art director, mechanical and printing limitations, and, most important, the intentions of the author.

A cover artist may accept a commission for one book or for a series of books (usually by the same author), or be under contract to the publisher to do a certain number of covers per year. Most artists meet with the art director to discuss each assignment; however, some highly experienced artists are given work over the phone and by mail.

During the initial meeting, the artist learns what portion of

Different realistic styles of Mitchell Hooks, commissioned by different publishers in the years 1951–62, a formative period for cover illustration:

Signet (1951).

Bantam (1952).

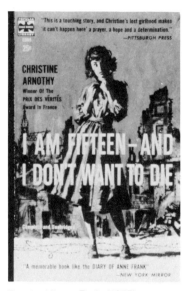

Popular Library Eagle (1957).

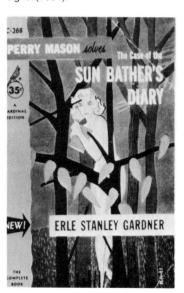

Pocket Books Cardinal (1958).

Dell (1960).

Gold Medal (1962).

the cover design is to be illustrated and receives a general layout of the cover. Generally prepared by the art director, the layout may be a quickly drawn sketch.

Often the cover artist will not read the book to be illustrated, especially if it belongs to a genre where a particular fictional writing formula is common, e.g., romances, gothics, and some Westerns. Once informed about the general plot and setting, the artist can paint a formula cover to complement the writing, one with all the necessary colors and clichés expected by wholesale and retail book buyers and by readers. This same practice, however, can inspire reader complaints when the cover art does not accurately reflect the book's content.

At Bantam Books in the late 1940s artists were given a paragraph summarizing an event described in the book and directed to illustrate the paragraph. This description often reappeared in the text, opposite the title page:

> High in a Manhattan penthouse . . . a disheveled girl—and a gun. Outside, the myriad lighted windows of the City— each hiding its own secret. . . .
> She stands for the Sins of New York . . . and the Sinners. [From Milton Crane, ed., *Sins of New York,* Bantam #786, 1950] [See Plate 12.]

For most books, however, particularly bestselling reprints and original lead titles, the artist needs a fuller taste of the content. Artists generally feel a responsibility to the author and read at least part of the book before beginning work on the cover. The more important the title, the more likely the artist is to read not only the book itself but also to study other background material that relates to the text.

The artist often then offers the publisher one or more rough sketches. These usually show the general scene and the positioning of characters. Recommendations for colors may be made at this time. Artists usually prepare these sketches by using pictures from books they have researched, clippings they have saved, commercial photo archives, and people they have photographed themselves or in modeling studios that specialize in paperback work.

Photographic covers are widely used for nonfiction and media

Publishers sometimes print separate covers for different markets. This photo of Mickey Spillane's wife, while fine for male- and adult-oriented retail stores, was not seen as suitable for family-oriented stores like supermarkets. Thus, two covers were designed (1972).

Cover Art and Design

92

tie-in covers; relatively few, however, are found on contemporary and genre fiction. Occasionally, the covers of important titles or series of fictional works are illustrated with photographs. These often display provocative females and are slanted toward a male readership. Photographers who are able to capture the sweet romantic feeling of some of the white covers of the 1960s also find their work used as centerpieces for softcover designs. Today, art directors believe that photography can be used successfully, especially on romantic novels, if it contains some of the soft-edged mistiness of cover drawings. The airbrush, inherited from magazine and advertising illustration of the 1930s, is used for both photographic and painted covers, to achieve the softness, color transitions, and blends characteristic of so many cover illustrations.

With or without photographic models, the cover artist then prepares a comprehensive drawing, a last step before the actual finished artwork. At a minimum the comprehensive drawing shows the various figures to be included in the illustration, their positions on the cover, their color values, and some background scenery.

The final painting is usually a detailed rendition of the comprehensive drawing. On occasion, though, the artist may be asked to make additional changes in the final illustration—a tilt of a head or the color of a dress, for example.

The more important the assignment, the more money the artist receives; talent and experience also influence the fee. A job illustrating front, back, and spine, for instance, pays more than front-cover artwork alone. Cover artists may receive on any one assignment as little as a few hundred dollars to as much as $5,000 or more.

During the early years of mass market book publishing, publishers usually bought artwork outright from artists. Seldom was there a formal contract that covered other uses or disposition of artwork. Today it is more common for publishers to lease original artwork for reproduction and for the artist to retain ownership. The stiff New York City sales tax, which is applied to the sale of a commissioned piece, is mainly responsible for this new arrangement. The original artwork is photographed and returned to the artist. Color negatives, color transparencies, and color plates then become the media from which the cover is printed. After manufacture all are preserved by the publisher and the printer for future reprints.

This lease arrangement for cover art is also preferred by artists who have been discovered by collectors of realistic art. Through gallery sales artists may equal or even double the money received from a publisher for their art. An artist can also generate income from secondary rights reproduction when the artwork is used for posters or by foreign publishers in their editions.

For a reissue, a publisher sometimes takes a portion of the original art and combines it with a new typographic design and color scheme. More often, though, a new piece of original artwork, usually in a different style and from a different artist, is commissioned for a reissue. Many long-standing paperback titles have had six or more different cover designs (see Plates 13a–i).

The speed with which an artist can complete a cover illustration varies greatly from illustrator to illustrator and depends on the size and difficulty of the work. Although artists have been known to complete a job overnight, most take a week to a month to finish a cover. Perhaps no one in the history of mass market cover illustration drew faster than Baryé Phillips, once dubbed the "King of the Paperbacks." Phillips, whose work is strongly identified with Fawcett Gold Medal covers of the 1950s, consistently turned out four finished paintings a week (see page 124 and Plate 7b).

Artwork can be done in different media, but fast-drying acrylics are usually preferred to oils. Generally, art directors do not require a particular size or scale. Almost all paintings are executed much larger than final cover dimensions, with the original art reduced to the desired size in the platemaking process. This reduction often eliminates minor imperfections in the original art, but it also tends to muddy detail and subtleties captured by the artist on canvas. Experienced artists anticipate this and paint accordingly.

Early paperback covers were printed by letterpress machinery, but beginning in the early 1950s a trend toward the use of offset lithography developed. Offset printing plates are cheaper to prepare and give better reproduction quality. Because images are sharper and colors truer, the finished product is more faithful to the original artwork. Today, all major paperback printers have offset equipment, and covers are printed by this method almost exclusively. For particularly difficult or fine reproduction, publishers often select a printer separate from the book manufacturer and arrange to have covers shipped to the text manufacturer for binding.

With the submission and acceptance of the finished painting the cover artist's involvement with the book project is completed. Once delivered, it becomes the job of the art director's staff to fit other parts of the layout around the art: title, author's name, and blurbs. Cover artists may be asked to look at a final design or press proof, but more often they see the fully executed design for the first time in retail stores. Artists find the study of the publisher's design built around their artwork and displayed alongside competitive titles a worthwhile, if sometimes disheartening, exercise. The realities and compromises made in designing the book, as well as effects never anticipated, come sharply into focus at the point of sale.

9
The Point of Sale

The point of sale is the retail outlet where a paperback book and its potential purchaser come together. Initially, however, a book must first sell itself to the publisher's own sales force and to buyers for bookstores. The cover plus a short synopsis of the book are often the only pieces of information carried by the sales rep for titles that are not lead titles or blockbusters. With these tools the sales representative tries to solicit appropriately large orders from buyers. The publisher's sales force must themselves be convinced of the marketing potential of a new title if their enthusiasm is to be projected to wholesale or large-volume retail buyers. In both situations the book's cover design is the attention-grabber.

If the buyer is impressed by the cover art, it also bodes well for the book's reception by the public. The larger the buyer's order, the greater the likelihood that the book will receive ample display space. Cover price is also involved here. A publisher estimates at various points during the life of a manuscript the number of copies that eventually will be printed, but only after the major book wholesale and retail chain-store accounts have given their orders is a cover price finally set and a first printing order determined. The greater the initial sales order, the more copies are likely to be printed; and the more copies printed, the lower the unit cost for each book manufactured. By combining the unit price with overhead, royalties, and advertising and promotion budgets, the publisher can estimate the break-even point of sales for a particular title.

Category books are bought much like magazines. Using past sales experience the wholesale and retail buyer, as well as the publisher, can usually estimate sales with great accuracy. Cover design seldom moves a buyer to place extraordinarily large orders for category titles; however, buyers can be turned off completely by designs they do not like and, as a result, they order fewer copies.

Reprints of bestsellers and "hype" books (books with mediocre to poor hardcover sales records, which the paperback publisher nevertheless believes to have the ingredients of a softcover bestseller) are challenges for salesmen. With each type the goal of the sales representative is to solicit from each buyer as large an order as possible. Heavy media advertising and promotion are promised by the publisher for these kinds of books. A publisher has to be sure of at least two things when releasing an important book: that copies are on display in quantities large enough to attract a reader's attention, thus reinforcing the expensive advertising and promotion, and that sufficient inventories are available locally to restock the title quickly once the book begins to sell.

Most media campaigns last only a few weeks. After that, the publisher generally relies on word of mouth to encourage sales. However, once it has been established that sales of a particular title are taking off, the publisher often renews the media campaign, sometimes on a much larger scale than originally. At the same time, sales representatives are directed to actively solicit wholesale and retail reorders.

The mid-list book's cover art can be more important to its initial sale than blockbuster or hype titles because it does not have the sales assistance of an extensive promotional campaign. For a book buyer unfamiliar with their titles, authors, or subjects, books on a publisher's mid-list are the easiest to order in token quantities or to ignore completely. Publishers are frequently accused by booksellers of regularly issuing certain titles for quantitative purposes to fill out their monthly list of new releases to ensure that their customary retail display pockets are filled from month to month. Whether or not this is in fact true, successful sales for titles that are not blockbuster or lead titles often depend on the cover art. For both sales representative and buyer the quality of the cover art is frequently the most tangible evidence of a publisher's faith in a book's sales potential.

There is general agreement among mass market publishers that readers of mass market paperbacks belong to one of two general types: occasional readers, who generally purchase books on impulse; and habitual readers of certain categories of books, who purposefully browse through displays of softcover books for new titles.

Publishers who specialize in romance and science fiction have very clear pictures of their habitual buyers. Harlequin has built its success on the discovery that the regular readers of their romantic fiction are a hard core. Addicted to this brand-name literature, they will sometimes buy a whole month's worth of new releases at once.

Betty Ballantine describes science fiction fans as

> the publisher's dream readers. Knowledgeable, articulate, informed and self-propelled, they will aggressively seek out books they want, and talk endlessly to one another about their favorite authors and artists. And write endlessly in their fanzines to one another about them. There is no other reading interest (although interest is too mild a word) which has provoked such a cohesive, organized group of devotees—a phenomenon which amply justifies the word they use to describe themselves, for they are truly fan-atics.

The paperback display rack with face-out cover designs attracts both habitual and occasional readers. The habitual reader needs little incentive to look. All this reader asks is that books be segregated by category so that he or she can quickly locate titles of interest. Such readers have been known to buy succeeding editions of the same book because of the fresh cover art placed on a newly reissued title.

In contrast, the occasional reader must be pulled to the book rack by its location and attractiveness. Once there, the publicity and advertising generated by the publisher interact with the cover designs on display. The browser, facing in effect hundreds of small billboards, reaches to examine those titles that are familiar and flash a promise of entertainment, escape, or knowledge; titles that offer something found pleasurable in the past or that may be helpful in the future. The cover encourages the buyer to select the book from the rack, inspect the front cover more carefully, turn it over and read the promotional copy on the back cover, and, finally, look inside for additional description, promotional copy, and reviews. At this moment of truth, publishers believe that even the feel of a book can aid its purchase. For very important books a smooth cover stock is often specified; on this smooth surface various spray finishes can be applied, giving the paperback cover a pleasing, often sensual feel.

Off the rack and into the hands of the reader the book's cover design achieves, at the point of sale, the goal intended by the art director and cover artist: to attract, compel examination, and inspire purchase.

10
Evolution

Like paperback books themselves, cover illustrations trace their roots back to the mid-nineteenth century. In England the yellowbacks (which at times also had pink, green, blue, or gray wrappers) attracted potential purchasers by the woodcut prints on their front covers. After 1852 these line illustrations frequently were tinted. The Beadle Dime Novels (see page 29), which were published a few years later, also used woodcuts on their orange covers to prompt readers, especially soldiers in the Civil War, to purchase them. As cheap paperback libraries evolved in the last quarter of the nineteenth century, illustrations became more sophisticated by including more detail and some color. In the early twentieth century, Street & Smith continued to issue softcover books with illustrated covers long after most publishers had stopped publishing cheap paperback editions.

Early Pocket Books covers were drawn in styles reminiscent of the hardcover dust jackets of the day. The concept of dust jackets on books is itself a relatively new idea. The earliest-known English dust jackets appeared in 1833; they were typographical in design and protected hardcover books. Jackets with color illustrations, engendered by the flashy success of the nineteenth-century paperback libraries and the newsstand fiction of Street & Smith, did not gain popularity with American hardcover trade-book publishers until the 1920s.

Twentieth-century Tauchnitz, Albatross (see page 25), and

Bantam (1946). Cover illustrated by Rafael Palacios; dust jacket by Paul Koloda.

early Penguin editions (see page 27) all carried dust jackets. Displaying strictly typographic designs, they were identical to the paper cover they surrounded. These paperback dust jackets aimed not so much to catch the attention of the reader as to reveal the nature and content of the book. Even after Pocket Books' jacketless success, an occasional American mass market paperback appeared with a jacket. These were 1940s reissues of previously published titles. They were freshened by newly designed jackets that hid an earlier cover design, which the publisher deemed less attractive.

The early Pocket Books covers also had a juvenile appearance about them, as if they were drawn by children to appeal to children. However, even among the first series of ten there were portents of things to come. Samuel Butler's provocatively titled classic, *The Way of All Flesh,* shows a proper-looking young man staring at a not-so-proper young woman in a décolleté gown and red-striped tights (see page 39). The first half of the 1940s saw few examples of objectionable covers. The mildly sensational covers of Pocket's editions of *Appointment in Samarra* (see page 55) and *The Werewolf of Paris* (see Plate 8a) were exceptions. Another occurred in 1941, when Pocket unveiled the most suggestive cover it had yet issued and pasted it around Zola's *Nana.* The tainted heroine appears full figure on the cover, resplendent in a diaphanous gown, in which she "flaunted her reign over Parisian society." It was spectacularly successful. (See Plates 15a–b.)

Despite public protests, *Nana* went back to press twelve times after its initial Pocket appearance and became one of the most popular books in the armed services during World War II. While Pocket did not follow up *Nana*'s artistic success with similar covers on other reprints, the new cover that appeared on the postwar reissue was equally provocative. Pocket Books defended both wrapper designs as accurately portraying the book. Later in the late 1940s, and throughout most of the 1950s, official and quasi-official groups and authorities attacked less accurate cover representations with a storm of adjectives synonymous with the word "salacious."

During World War II Avon's cover art took its cue from Pocket Books, and, as previously noted, ended in court for this form of flattery. Popular Library and Dell used more sophisticated approaches, employing symbolism and surrealism to get across the message of the mystery stories that dominated their lists. Penguin's American branch, with a more varied list of publications, moved in five years from purely typographic covers to full-color cover illustrations—an evolution that its parent company in England would take twenty-five years to duplicate.

As early as 1942, Pocket Books adopted a front-cover format that gave their books an even more distinctive look. Color illustrations were framed in double borders, which ran around all four sides of the cover. At the close of World War II Penguin returned permanently to their original 7¼″ length, and front-cover drawings were designed with headbands and footbands. About this same time Avon literally drew picture frames around their front-cover drawings. The borders prevented artwork from bleeding onto the spines and back covers but encouraged fully painted, full-color solutions to illustration assignments. Cover artists often used every inch of the "canvas" provided by the publisher's cover format. (See Plates 14a–d.)

In 1946 not only was there an expansion in variety and quantity of softcover publication lists but there were also major changes in their design. At this time publishers became convinced that they were competing as much with magazines as with hardcover books. Consequently, paperbacks were increasingly outfitted as "miniature magazines," to do battle for display space in the newsstands, cigar stores, and drugstores of postwar America.

Cover styles were influenced by cover and story illustrations of slick magazines like *The Saturday Evening Post* and *Collier's,* or the outrageous and sensational pulps which crowded periodical display racks. The slick styles caught the fancy of male and female buyers, but the pulp covers appealed almost exclusively to a masculine audience.

Pocket Books and Bantam generally adopted the slick magazine style. Avon, Popular, and most other newly established imprints mimicked the more forceful and daring pulp-style illustration. Regardless of style, artwork took a more realistic bend, details became more important and figures more representational, as opposed to decorative or symbolic.

At about this time Robert Jonas, a designer and artist, began creating expressionistic covers for Penguin and Pelican titles.

Penguin (1946). Illustrated by
Robert Jonas.

This style, not widely imitated by other publishers, continued into the 1950s on Mentor Books, successor imprint to the American Pelicans. However, a Jonas cover in another style, the rather crude illustration of a backwoods cabin framed through a knothole for Erskine Caldwell's *God's Little Acre,* gained wide attention. The book became a runaway bestseller, and the knothole cover that promised forbidden insights into Southern comforts was credited with stimulating much of the sales. The peephole device, placed within the rather rigid front-cover frame design, gave birth to literally hundreds of paperbound keyholes, wall chinks, and assorted spyholes. For many readers the Jonas knothole has become a symbol of paperback publishing.

James Avati's fully painted illustrations, which began in 1949, were ideally suited for the bordered cover formats used by Signet and others. Avati's unadorned realistic style, combined with his controlled shadings of browns and grays, gave paperback cover art an honesty and emotional depth that the pulp-style and magazine-style illustrations lacked. His publisher called them "Rembrandt-like." Comprehensive in design, they offered a stage to the viewer on which the most dramatic scene of the book was memorably portrayed. Foreground and background items were painted in detail, each revealing a facet of the book's character and setting. Most startling were the faces of the figures illustrated. Often not handsome, beautiful, or even pretty, they were real faces one could meet on a hometown street, alive with emotion and feeling. (See Plates 16a–d.)

Avati gave fresh expression to commercial illustration. The New American Library, publishers of Signet fiction, discovered that Avati's style of painting sold books. Independent wholesalers were likely to buy more books and display a title longer if Avati's signature was on the cover. Even books with very successful designs, like Jonas's *God's Little Acre,* were reissued with Avati's cover art. His style was the first pure "paperback art." For a half dozen very formative years in the history of the major paperback houses, Avati and "Avati-like" covers dominated display racks. His influence on other paperback artists was enormous: NAL, as well as other softcover publishers, demanded direct imitations of the "Avati look" from commissioned illustrators.

Adaptations of Avati's realistic style were ideally suited for sexual exploitation. Throughout the late 1940s it was obvious to softcover publishers that the sensational styles of pulp illustrations sold certain books: Westerns, detective novels, and, especially, light fiction. From out of those dark and somber hotel rooms and city-street backgrounds came women in every state of undress imaginable, pursued by roaring guns and raging men. (See Plates 17a–d.) Avati's moody realism, when combined with harsher pulp illustrative themes, often produced exaggerated and frequently misleading cover pieces.

Of all the facets of paperback art to emerge over the past forty years, the most constant is the sexual theme. The heavy-handed, pulp-inspired cover art of male-oriented paperbacks of the 1940s and 1950s portrayed the female figure in sordid poses to the point of being ludicrous. Early artists were often required to "have something show," and their women's apparel came apart at the seams and in a lot of other places. In December 1952 the House Select Committee on Current Pornographic Materials held hearings that focused in part on various paperback publishing practices. The male paperback buyer of the time, however, might well have believed that the committee's concern would have been better directed at design defects in the ladies' garment industry. Even the most casual observer of cover designs must have wondered why the shoulder straps of women's dresses and brassieres were always loose, slipping, or undone.

Innocence was seldom portrayed in a female subject, and even when it was, virtue was betrayed by the angle of a leg or a bare shoulder or a subtly carnal glance. Males appearing on these sensational paperbacks seemed only to get in the way: seldom the central figures in the illustrations, they often strategically blocked a provocative anatomical feature of their female counterpart.

These two-fisted, double-breasted, four-color broadsides, subject to editorial attack, police raids, boycotts, and government investigation, instilled in the American popular mind a sleazy image of paperback books. *Saturday Review* created and defined the verb "to paperback" as: "to undress an idea or a book, but especially a book, and to varnish it with questionable taste." This image remained through the 1950s; time and fresher, subtler paperback designs began to erase it in the 1960s and 1970s. Though far less exaggerated, the style of basic figure representa-

THIS PAGE AND OPPOSITE.
Examples of Bantam's search for
fresher cover designs in the 1950s:

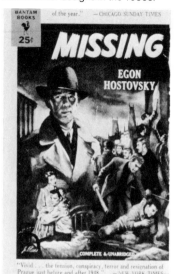

1953, illustrated by Joseph Polseno.

1956, illustrated by Mitchell Hooks.

Cover Art and Design

104

tion has nonetheless not changed from the late 1940s slick maga-zine styles. The women are slim, blond, pale, and inordinately beautiful; men are dark-haired and dark-skinned, roguishly handsome and virile. Both sexes are painted realistically, often with almost photographic detail, a combination of the ideal and the real. Yet within this combination is a range of styles that range from the pop art of the Harlequin romances to the super-detailed realism of a Remington-inspired Western cover.

Front-cover artwork was only one contributor to the turmoil softcover publishers experienced in the first half of the 1950s. Authors were demanding higher royalties; original publication imprints threatened to undermine established relationships be-tween hardcover and softcover publishers; production costs were rising; book returns were piling up in publishers' and whole-salers' warehouses; censors were attacking the whole industry. Yet sales were never greater. While each publisher felt the need to duplicate the obviously successful design features of competi-tors (most publishers had adopted the longer 7⅛″ height by this time), including cover art that sold, segregation by publisher im-print remained the usual display arrangement at the retail level.

Publishers continued to maintain individual looks by placing cover illustrations in a format design—standard front, spine, and back cover bordered layouts into which the illustration, typogra-phy, and promotional blurbs were placed—unique to each im-print. The publisher's name, logo, series titles, and motto all had predetermined spots on the front or back cover. Each publisher tended to select a certain color or color combination for the front cover which, together with the color stain sprayed on at the end of manufacture, further aided identification. Yellow, for instance, dominated the front covers and spines of Fawcett's Gold Medal titles, and page edges were stained yellow or orange at the top. The edge stains, besides aiding imprint identification, also dis-guised the yellowing of brittle, high-pulp-content paper. Today's "free sheet" book papers (free of wood pulp, which quickens dis-coloration) are seldom stained.

Bantam appears to have been unsatisfied with its format, how-ever. Throughout the first half of the 1950s, the company experi-mented with several format-design changes in its various series. Besides using wraparound art (illustrations that bleed over to the back cover), they lengthened the format of their standard twenty-five-cent series to 7⅛″. For a time they adopted a framed area for a full-color painting similar to the Signet imprint. By the mid-1950s, however, Bantam artists were not required to cover every inch inside the frame. Background details could be omitted; blank space was not always filled in; and details of central figures were sometimes left out. A series of vignettes rather than single scenes from the book was often used; sketches replaced full-color figures, and outlines were softened. Although the artwork was still representational, the illustrations were freer, more inventive, and less finished. Often resembling rough preliminary sketches rather than finished paintings, these drawings left more to the imagination than the literal, Avati pulp styles, leading *House Beautiful* magazine to observe that "book covers, like dresses, are flimsier than they used to be."

Concurrent with this graphic evolution was another develop

1956, illustrated by Mitchell Hooks.

1953, illustrator unknown.

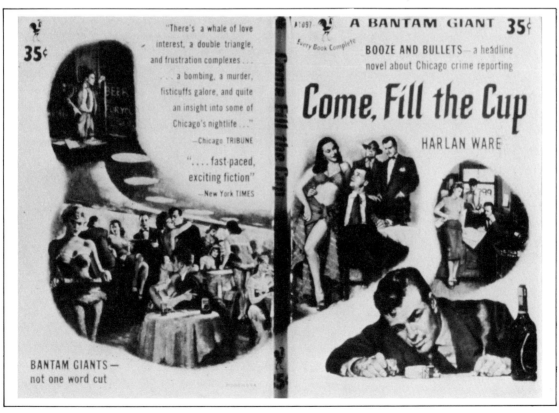

ment at the detail end of the paperback distribution spectrum. Booksellers were beginning to realize that softcover book sales increased significantly if titles were arranged by subject matter rather than by publisher imprint. This trend was accelerated by the explosion, beginning in the mid-1950s, of new paperback imprints; 90 percent or more were introduced by hardcover trade-book publishers and university presses. By 1965 approximately four hundred trade and mass market softcover imprints were being issued. For bookstores serious about selling paperbacks, it became impractical to arrange them other than by subject.

The end of publisher displays at the retail level also spelled the end of inflexible formats. This new trend toward subject category arrangement meant that each new book had to compete for sales independent of the other publications of the same imprint. Readers were no longer attracted to the Signet racks by their handsomely framed front-cover designs, lined up headband to headband, row after row, in harmonious uniformity. Rather, they selected their purchases from a mixture of imprints with conflicting designs and styles of cover art.

Each title, then, had to stand out, to become a miniature billboard communicating its message in competition with surrounding titles. A poster style of cover design evolved, compatible with the unfinished style of the illustrations Bantam had been using. Borders, frames, headbands, and footbands began to disappear from the formats of all publishers. Images bled off all sides of the front cover. Author, title, and front-cover blurbs were moved around more freely instead of being positioned at the top of the cover design.

Illustrated images took up a smaller portion of the front cover, leaving backgrounds of solid color. Before this trend there had been no such thing as a red cover or a blue cover; there were only the dominant colors within a cover artist's painting. The poster style, de-emphasizing fully painted covers, in contrast made the cover-stock hue an important consideration.

As a result, various theories of color appropriateness have developed. There is little overall agreement, but the primary colors of red, yellow, and blue seem to be favored generally by designers. Westerns often appear with brown backgrounds; horror tales and gothics, black or dark blue. Purple and green are seldom used, and in some houses have been proscribed altogether.

Gold and silver, generally not used as background colors in the early years of mass market publishing, are now frequently used by cover designers. Besides using metallic cover stocks, designers often emboss or stamp metallic foil on cover titles or figures. The first example of systematic use of gold occurred in 1950, when Pocket Books introduced the thirty-five-cent Cardinal Editions; gold borders were designed for the front and back covers. Soon imitated in several competing publisher formats, Pocket Books later boasted, "This lavish use of gold brought a new note of richness to the paperbound field."

White, however, has become today's most frequently used color, especially for lead titles on a publisher's list. White covers were found objectionable in the early years of paperback publishing by people on the selling end—sales representatives, wholesalers, and retailers—because they "showed the dirt too much." Very dark covers, incidentally, are disliked even today because they readily show scratches and wear.

Objections to white background covers were overcome in the mid-1960s with Bantam's great success with *The Harrad Experiment* and *Boys and Girls Together*. (See Plates 18a and b.) Their subtly emotional cover paintings jumped out from wire racks and demanded attention from prospective buyers. Paperback publishers were not in the least hesitant to duplicate Bantam's white-cover successes. "Soon every publisher was issuing books in white covers until the customer, poised before the rack, was threatened with snow blindness," Bantam historian Clarence Petersen observed.

Since the early 1960s publishers have not tried to set a standard design format, except for specific series that are predictably shelved together at the retail level. Rather, certain design innovations have appeared, the result of one or more successful publications by a particular publisher. For a time these styles dominate a larger percentage of the publisher's editions and establish a look imitated by competitors, as happened with Bantam's white-cover look. In the second half of the 1970s, for instance, Avon's historical romance logotypes gave a fresh look to books written by and published for women (see Plate 19), establishing an "Avon look." In time, however, these new looks date and wear out from sheer repetition, and are replaced by fresh inventions.

11
Genre and Other Designs

Each category of popular literature has evolved its own set of cover elements and clichés whose use is more or less required. The best known and most easily recognized of these are the "formula" covers for gothic romances. Throughout the 1960s and early 1970s this category demanded that a long-haired beautiful young woman appear on a fully painted cover. In the foreground she would be framed by a tortured landscape, while a forbidding mansion or castle loomed behind, a single light always beaming from an upper window. The dominant color was usually dark blue. (See Plates 20a and b.)

A contrast to the cliché gothics is the variety of cover treatments for the first popular paperback genre, mysteries. Early mysteries usually portrayed a victim and a murder weapon on the cover. Hands, skulls, and skeletons were other popular illustrative devices borrowed from digest mystery magazines. (See Plates 21a–e.) As this genre became more popular, more subcategories appeared, such as detective fiction and suspense and spy thrillers, along with the original classic murder mysteries. The nature of the central character frequently determined the nature of the cover art—witness the sadistic pulp covers of Mickey Spillane's hardboiled fiction of the 1950s, as brutal as Mike Hammer himself. While the heavy-handed sadism has been lightened of late, the detective-adventure exploits (and exploiters) of the 1970s have carried on this violent tradition with cover designs dense with sex and camp humor. The gun and knife are now explicit phallic symbols, while in the 1940s and 1950s this aspect was largely unrecognized or subliminal.

Suspense and horror tales, like the gothic novels to which they are related, almost always require dark covers. Illustrations are often small and symbolic, with spot drawings frequently centered on the front cover. The Bantam cover for *The Exorcist* started a wave in this style, which was subsequently refined by the Signet edition of Stephen King's *Salem's Lot*. The jet-black front cover contained no typography for author or title, simply an embossed head of a woman with a single drop of red blood suspended from her lower lip.

Among fiction categories, cover art for the classic Western has evolved the least through the years. Two strong traditions have dominated the field. The fine-art school of Frederic Remington and Charles Russell has influenced two generations of cover artists and inspired much of the art now appearing on Western paperback covers. Lovingly realistic in detail, this style of illustration seems to bring out the finest in a cover artist. Once mastered, it has encouraged many illustrators to forsake commercial art commissions and devote their energies to studio art. The other trend in Western cover art is the familiar shoot-'em-up, ride-'em-out pulp style. This requires illustrative skills equal to the fine-art school and is dominated by the exaggerated realism of firing guns and steaming horses in dusty cattle towns. (See Plates 22a and b.) Until recently, a female face was seldom found on these covers. But the rise of the adult Western, in which a cowboy knows the difference between a girl and a horse and acts accordingly, has given rise to cover art themes not unlike those of the detective/adventure school, but in Western garb.

A contrast to the slow evolution of the Western cover is the unchecked growth of fantasy literature, especially the science fiction category. The very early science fiction covers published by Ace and Ballantine in the mid-1950s were, like most general fiction, illustrated either in the slick or pulp magazine tradition. A breakthrough occurred when Ballantine began commissioning the unique work of Richard Powers. Although not widely imitated today, Powers's abstract art signaled in the late 1950s that artists could experiment with this category of literature (see Plates 23a–d and 24a and b).

The spaceships of the early pulps still abound on science fic-

An adult Western cover (Jove, 1980), illustrated by veteran cover artist George Gross.

Genre and Other Designs

109

tion covers; however, the rise of all kinds of fantasy literature has allowed cover art to range in style from the quaint juvenile charm of a Hildebrandt brothers' underground world to the macho sword-and-sorcery epics of Frank Frazetta and others. Science fiction has also been an almost exclusively male-dominated field: few women write in the genre, few illustrate it, and until recently it was believed that few read it. Perhaps this accounts in part for science fiction having the most blatantly sexist covers of any fiction category.

Just as it is known that Westerns, detective/adventure, and science fiction/fantasy appeal chiefly to male audiences, romances and their various categories appeal almost exclusively to female readers. (One paperback art director regards the ideal design of a romance cover as akin to that of an attractive box of chocolates: a package hard not to pick up and sample.) The second half of the 1970s witnessed the advent and triumph of the historical romance. Avon books began publishing a series of original historical novels in the literary traditions of *Forever Amber* and *Gone with the Wind* aimed at the woman who has never been afraid to ask Dr. Reuben. Avon not only developed and raised this genre to the status of a blockbuster bestseller but also gave it an appearance that inspired new designs in several fiction and nonfiction categories. Built around the standard clutch pose—a long-haired woman wrapped in an embrace with a darker-skinned man—these covers feature exotic backgrounds and flowered foregrounds that often float around the spine and onto the back cover (see Plates 25a and b).

The typographical elements of the front cover of these romances are integrated into the artwork, rather than superimposed on the illustration. Equal to the illustrative clichés of the painting, the typography or "logotype" signals the reader and conveys the promise of untamed adventure and wild romance. The titles of these books usually underscore this avowal of abandon with strong image words like "rape," "passion," and "lust." ("Fantastically active titles," one publisher calls them.) They are often tempered by the contrasting innocence of the author's name, "Faith," "Bright," and "Goode."

Simultaneous with the growth of the historical romance in paperback publishing has been the rise of the paperback sagas and multivolume series. Generally treated as lead titles, both genres appeal to a wide spectrum of readers through their combination of history, adventure, and romance. The sagas are usually inordinately lengthy, and big books have always been a problem for publishers. On the one hand they are expensive to manufacture because they require more paper and are more difficult to bind. Their thickness also reduces the number of books that can be carried in the slot of a rack display. On the other hand, a thicker book may appear to justify the higher price tag the book probably carries. Thick books also appeal to readers looking for a story in which to lose themselves, "big, juicy reads" in trade argot.

Better perhaps than a single thick book is a series of books by the same author. Usually tracing the turbulent rise of a family through several generations, with important historical events as backdrop, fiction series began to dominate paperback lists at the end of the 1970s. The cover art for this latest editorial phenomenon was pioneered by John Jakes's Kent family adventures. Elements were included to attract both the male and the female reader in a sequence of vignettes containing the illustrative clichés we have come to recognize on adventure, Western, and romance covers. Shelved together, a multivolume series can command considerable display space and overwhelm nearby competitors with the promise of many hours of escape reading.

A series like the Kent family chronicles carries a unique risk, however. The cover art for these books, developed and published over a period of years, can become dated or, because of imitation by competition, tired. Yet in order to retain earlier readers and preserve the attractiveness of a multiple-copy display, the publisher cannot afford to change the design radically.

Sheer quantity makes the standard design formats of classics imprints more difficult to change. In 1954 Pocket Books published its first classics titles under the Pocket Library imprint. By 1960 each major paperback house was issuing a series of public domain and backlist bestsellers aimed at school and college classroom adoption. These mass market classics series took their cover cues from early English Pelicans, as well as from the more recent trade paperback series such as Doubleday's Anchor and Knopf's Vintage, which used recognized artists like Leonard Baskin and Edward Gorey. The cover artists for these classics editions were offered, within a set front-cover series format, greater artistic latitude than usual. Classics series carried what *The New York Times* described as "discreet covers"—cover art literally designed not to offend even very sensitive tastes and to improve the tarnished image of the mass market paperback houses.

The Signet Classics series is generally acknowledged as the most successfully designed and illustrated set of mass market classics. For the series New American Library commissioned illustrators working in different illustrative styles, many of whom had never before painted paperback covers. Covers for the Signet Classics Shakespeare series were illustrated by Milton Glaser, who had earlier designed trade paperbacks as well as Dell's Laurel classics. During the first half of the 1960s the Shakespeare series, as well as the Signet Classics series as a whole, received numerous design and illustration awards (see Plates 26a and b).

A more recent innovation in paperback series has been the development of uniform designs for the works of an author. Paperback publishers have from the start often had the same illustrator paint covers for different titles by the same author. Art directors and other publishing personnel then realized that similarly designed titles by the same author could produce a pleasing and attention-grabbing visual effect when arranged side by side. Despite the breakdown of publisher-arranged displays and the subsequent discarding of publisher formats, books by the same author, especially writers of fiction, continued to be shelved together. A publisher with several works by the same author on its list could create an author series by using the same general design and complementary pieces of art by the same illustrator (see Plates 27a and b).

The development of this kind of series requires enormous skill and sensitivity on the part of the artist and art director. For an author series to work well it must include for each title in the series certain symbols or moods inherent in the author's text that not only are faithful to the work but also visually compatible with the designs of other works in the series. With writers whose works fall into one of the numerous genres of popular fiction the challenge is not overwhelming. Series writers of contemporary fiction, however, are another story. Their books, which often vary widely in style, mood, and subject, must be

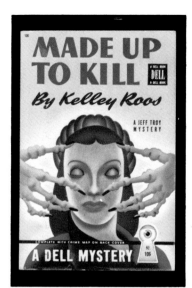

29a

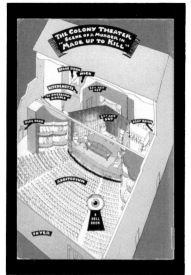

29b

29c

29d

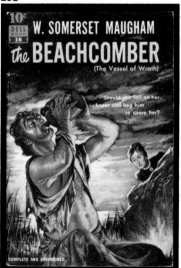

30a

30b

29. Dell front covers illustrated by
Gerald Gregg; back covers by
Ruth Belew:
29a. 1944. See p.47.

29d. 1948. See pp.47,122.

29b. 1944.

30. Dell Dimers published in 1951:
30a. Illustrated by Ralph DeSoto.

29c. 1948.

30b. Illustrated by Robert Stanley.
See p.123.

31a

31b

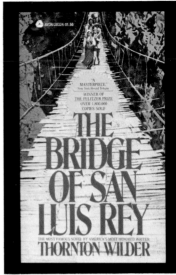

31c

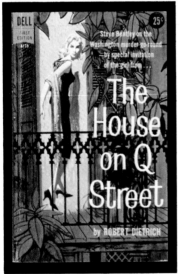

32a

32b

33a

31. Cover designs for *The Bridge of San Luis Rey:* **31a.** Charles Boni Paper Books (1929, sample edition). Designed and illustrated by Rockwell Kent. See p.32. 4^{15}/$_{16}$″x 7^{5}/$_{16}$″.

32. A pair of pseudonymous novels by Howard Hunt, both illustrated by Robert McGinnis: **32a.** 1959.

31b. Pocket Books (1939). Illustrated by Frank Lieberman.

32b. 1961. See p.125.

31c. Avon (1976). Illustrated by Robert McGinnis. See p.124.

33. Early covers for works by distinguished twentieth-century writers: **33a.** Pocket Books (1942). Illustrated by Harve Stein.

33b

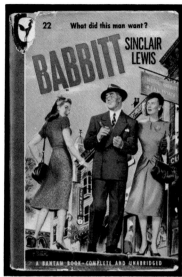

33c

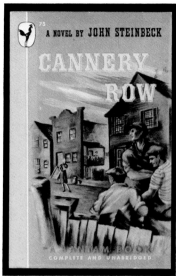

33d

33e

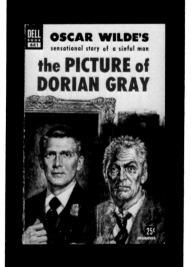

33f

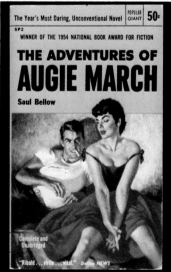

33g

33b. Bantam (1945). Illustrated by Edgard Cirlin.

33e. Avon (1952). Illustrator unknown.

33c. Bantam (1946). Illustrated by Bernard Barton.

33f. Dell (1953). Illustrated by Griffith Foxley.

33d. Bantam (1947). Illustrated by Lester Kohs.

33g. Popular Library (1953). Illustrator unknown. See p.125.

34a

34b

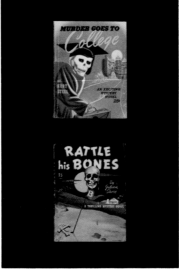

34c

35a–d

34. Double volumes of different designs: **34a.** Ace (1952). Illustrated by Norman Saunders.

34c. Signet (1978). *Web of Gunsmoke* illustrated by Longaron; *Ute Country* illustrated by Frank McCarthy. See pp.122,126.

35. Published by a variety of companies, paperback pulps flourished in the war years (all illustrators unknown). **35a.** Cornell Publishing Corporation (1944). 5'' x 6½''. **35b.** London Publishing Company (1944). 4¹⁵/₁₆'' x 6¹/₁₆''.

34b. Royal Giant (1953). Illustrated by Walter Papp. 5'' x 8''.

35c. Century Mystery (not dated). 5⁵/₁₆''x 7⁵/₈''. **35d.** Avon Murder Mystery Monthly (1942). 5¹/₄'' x 7⁵/₈'' See p.126.

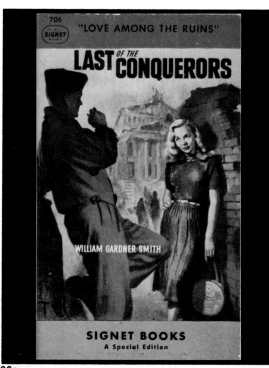

36a

36. Some significant illustrations of cover artist James Avati:
36a. Signet (1949). His first paperback cover.
36b. Signet (1953). The boy in this illustration stood as a symbol for a generation. The design and painting, however, were intensely disliked by Salinger and directly contributed to his transferring reprint rights to his works to Bantam in the early 1960s.
36c. Avon (1970 reissue). A favorite cover of the illustrator. See p.129.

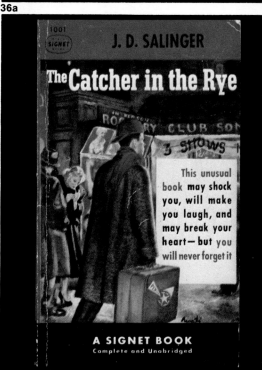

36b

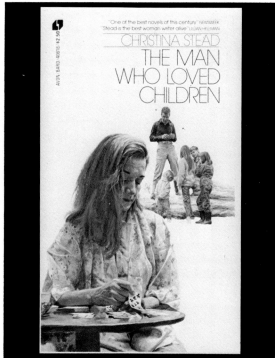

36c

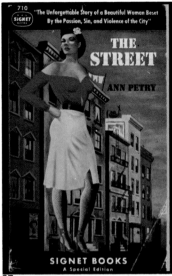

37a

37b

37c

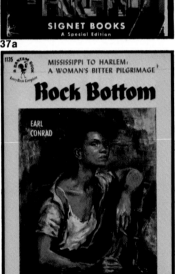

37d

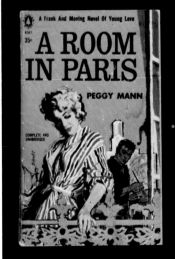

38a

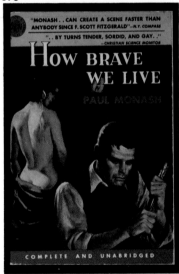

38b

37. Themes on early paperback covers: Blacks: **37a.** Signet (1949). Illustrated by Robert Jonas.

37d. Bantam (1953). Painting by Marian Greenwood, adapted for the book. See p.132.

37b. Bantam (1949). Illustrated by Robert Stanley.

38. Artists: **38a.** Popular Library (1956). Illustrated by Mitchell Hooks.

37c. Avon (1951). Illustrated by Ray Johnson.

38b. Avon (1952). Illustrator unknown.

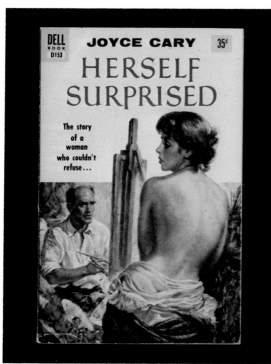

38c. Dell (1956). Illustrated by Raymond Pease.

38c

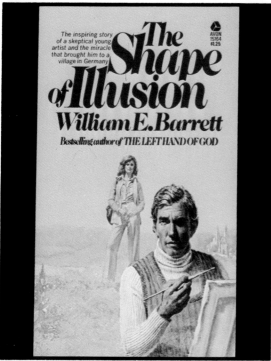

38d. Avon (1973). Illustrated by James Avati. See p.132.

38d

Following page
39. The Brooklyn Bridge. **39a.** Avon (1948). Illustrator unknown.
39b. Signet (1952). Illustrated by Rudy Nappi.
39c. Avon (1955). Illustrator unknown.
39d. Pocket Books (1955). Illustrated by John McClelland. See p.132.

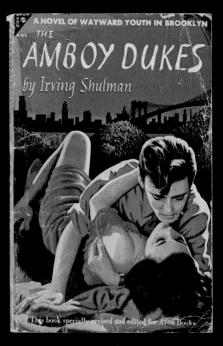

39a

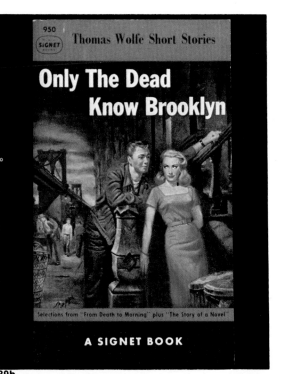

39b

39c

39d

designed with great care if the covers are to be valid. Typographic covers are frequently employed when the author is well known, or photographs may be used if the writer has an interesting face.

Some category authors outgrow a particular genre and find a wider general audience; their books often receive cover treatments devoid of genre clichés. Publishers also try to create new audiences. By putting a "woman's cover" on the reissue of a general work of fiction, a new readership may be reached, just as a sensational or sexy cover for the same work may attract a new male market.

A change in the public's perception of a writer can also result in a shift in cover treatment. Critical recognition and literary prizes frequently result in a new audience for a backlist author. Indeed, if a publisher owns rights to several books by that writer, reissues of the author's previous works may appear on newsstands, sporting fresh cover art. Popular literature that begins to attract sales in schools and colleges may end up appearing in the more prestigious "classics" formats.

Reissues of books in an author's series designed with similar formats can create other problems for an art director. In genre literature, where a writer has written a dozen or more pieces of formula fiction, the redesigned cover on a reissue may cause the faithful reader to buy the book a second time. To help prevent this, publishers, especially with romance and male-adventure author series, number the covers of the series. John D. MacDonald has long been aware of this problem and has used a subtitle device with his Travis McGee detective series. Each title in the series contains the name of a color: *The Deep Blue Good-Bye* or *A Deadly Shade of Gold.* The dominant color of each cover generally matches the color in the title.

The straight typographic cover highlighting the author's name if it is well known, or the title of the book, is an infrequently acknowledged inheritance from German and English paperback designs—used when it had to be used, but usually without great enthusiasm. In 1971, when Bantam published Erich von Däniken's *Chariots of the Gods?,* however, it specified a three-dimensional block letter, West Behemoth Shaded. This mechanically produced typeface had occasionally been used on earlier paper-

The popular display type, West Behemoth Shaded, designed by David West, appeared on this 1971 bestseller.

backs, but, like the bestseller it identified, it started a trend and continues to be widely specified for illustrated covers as well as for straight typographic covers.

Mechanically reproduced display type has been and remains the most common source for the typographical elements of paperback covers. However, the historical romances of the 1970s gave new popularity to hand-lettered, curlicue scripts for titles and author names (see Plate 19), which helped convey subliminal messages to potential buyers.

The editorial copy that appears on the front and back covers of all paperbacks, together with the illustration and typography, is a basic part of paperback design. Like the other two cover elements, the blurbs should attract and encourage the reader to examine the book in detail. Blurb writers are usually connected with the editorial departments of a publishing house. Increasingly, however, blurbs are written by freelancers who work for a set fee. The vocabulary at their disposal is limited. It is bordered on one side by superlatives, which stress the uniqueness of any given piece of literature, and on the other by descriptions that compare it with succesful bestsellers of the past.

Like the cover art, blurbs are overloaded with clichés, which can fizzle instead of enlighten. An inheritance from the pulps, where "zippy," "saucy," "fantastic," and "snappy" were overworked adjectives, blurb catchlines today routinely proclaim a book to be a "monumental saga of outrageous passion and fiery frenzy."

The blurbs from the 1940s and 1950s have a ring of innocent absurdity today that both delights and intrigues. Take for example the 1950 Avon front cover for Donald Henderson Clark's *Tawny:* "Can a girl from the slums win love and lucre on Park Ave.?" On the headband of Popular Library's 1951 reprint *Here Lies the Body* by Richard Burke, we are told even more succinctly that "a hot redhead meets a cold corpse."

By changing blurbs, colors, or cover illustrations, publishers occasionally issue lead titles with two or more design variations. The most common are those editions with different-colored cover stock or different spot illustrations on the front-cover design. Bantam Books pioneered this practice in the early 1970s, and it has been adopted on occasion by most softcover publishers. As with author series, this innovation often gets multiple-copy display on book racks. Multicovered editions also are visually effective when packaged in special point-of-sale display cartons. Publishers, uncertain of overall effectiveness, have used the device sparingly, fearing to blunt its impact if repeated too often. At least one publisher fears that the multiple covers may seem to be making different statements about the same book, "depriving the book of its authenticity." Reissues of books that have been given a multicovered first printing usually appear with only one design the next time around.

Paperback covers today reflect greeting-card designs. Although illustration styles are generally not as saccharine, the various mechanical gimmicks that appeared in the 1970s seemed to be directly inherited from that industry. Common devices are covers exhibiting such greeting-card practices as foil stamping, gold seals, embossing, die-cutting (holes in the front cover that reveal part of an illustration on the first page), step-back covers (the front cover is trimmed short so that the right-hand margin reveals a color band or part of the inside illustration), and cover gatefold and tipped-in gatefold (large illustrations that the reader folds out for a fuller poster effect). A few of the more exotic covers have even been scented, flocked, and sprayed with glitter.

Art directors are divided on the effectiveness of gimmick covers. Many are simply mechanical versions of Robert Jonas's peephole covers of the 1940s. All are designed to jump out at readers, encouraging them to examine the book more closely.

Foldouts and die-cuts are the mechanical solutions to getting the reader "under cover," i.e., to open up and examine the book's contents. More effective and less costly than the gimmick covers are traditional solutions featuring clean graphics, clever design, and provocative illustration, such as the unzipped cover of Erica Jong's *Fear of Flying*. Appealing to both sexes through purely visual images, such covers tease readers to look inside.

Today's paperback cover is the product of careful planning by dozens of people—freelance artists; photographers and designers; art directors and their staffs; publishers' editorial, production, and sales departments; the platemakers who compose the cover press plate; the printers who put it on cover stock; and the binders who attach it to the printed text. Successful cover de-

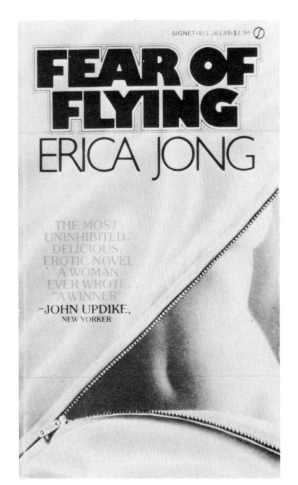

Unzipped cover art of the 1970s. LEFT: Signet (1973). Designed by Jim Plumeri, illustrated by Birney Lettick.
RIGHT: Warner (1978). Designed by Eugene Light, photo by Don Banks.

signs are imitated not only by other paperback publishing houses but by hardcover dust jackets and text illustrations as well. They have been copied in advertising, movie posters, record album covers, travel brochures, games and puzzles, and even cigarette packages. They have become an integral part of commercial advertising, the stamp of hyperbole for the entire American mass market paperback publishing industry.

Cover Art and Design

116

PART III
Collecting

Collecting

A magazine for readers of mystery stories once described two types of paperback book collectors:

> The first obtains books by their favorite authors. The second acquires any book that comes their way. These books are placed on shelves until there is no room left, then piled in boxes. Neither type will dispose of a book despite husbandly/wifely ire or warnings from a building inspector. Their only worry is which books to save in case of fire. [*Mystery Fancier,* Vol. 1, #6]

Bibliophile G. Thomas Tanselle sees much loftier ends for a collector, whom he describes as "a preserver of a cultural heritage, a pioneer who recognizes neglected areas and assembles the materials for *studying* them." But whatever the aims or practices, the results are clear. The acquisition of vintage paperback books is the fastest-growing area of book collecting in the United States.

Who are these collectors? They are the youth of the 1940s and 1950s rediscovering the discarded paperbacks of their adolescence, as well as younger generations literally raised from birth on paperbacks. The lure of the past, whether real or imagined, is common nourishment to them.

Once collecting is begun, however, a certain logic usually prevails. The novice collector must begin to sort out from the numerous varieties of paperback publishing those examples of the industry that appeal, are available, and promise to give some sort of lasting satisfaction. Part of this lasting satisfaction may relate to still another reason for collecting, that of monetary gain.

In November 1980, based on a review of a newly published price guide to vintage paperbacks, *Publishers Weekly* announced its "Ten Most-Wanted List of Paperbacks for Collectors."

1. *Reform School Girl* by Felice Swados. Diversey Romance Novel #1. $275 (digest size)
2. *The Dying Earth* by Jack Vance. Hillman #41. $60
3. *Marihuana* by William Irish. Dell 10¢ #11. $100
4. *The Case of the Dancing Sandwiches* by Frederic Brown. Dell 10¢ #33. $50
5. *Tarzan in the Forbidden City* by Edgar Rice Burroughs. Bantam of Los Angeles #23. $60
6. *The Shadow and the Voice of Murder* by Maxwell Grant. Bantam of Los Angeles #21. $60
7. *The Adventures of Superman* by George Lowther. Armed Services Edition #656. $40
8. *Junkie* by William Lee (pseudonym for William Burroughs) / *Narcotic Agent* by Maurice Helbront Ace #D-15. $100
9. *The Adventures of Sam Spade* by Dashiell Hammett. Bestseller Mystery #50. $30 (digest size)
10. *Lost Horizon* by James Hilton. Pocket Books #1. $100

Even assuming the books are in finest condition, no two collectors of paperbacks would agree on the titles or the amounts noted on the list. Nevertheless, these published prices go far to dispel the image of the paper-covered title as the Kleenex of the book trade.

APPROACHES TO COLLECTING

Paperbacks lend themselves to being collectible. First, they are widely available, turning up wherever secondhand items are sold, at thrift shops, swap shops, antique stores, used-furniture stores, flea markets, barn and garage sales, and library book sales. Naturally, they also are found in secondhand-book stores and in the paperback exchanges now popping up around the United States.

In recent years fiction genres like Westerns, mysteries, science fiction, and fantasy have acquired stables of fans who attend conventions and publish fanzines. The exhibits at these "cons," as the meetings are called, and dealer listings in fan publications also are sources for buying or trading paperbacks, as well as pulp magazines and comics. (See the "Further Reading" section at the end of this book for the names of publications aimed principally at softcover book collectors.)

Sending lists of desired publications ("want lists") to book dealers who advertise in these publications is an efficient way to fill gaps in one's collection. Many booksellers issue sales catalogs that one can regularly receive either by paying a small subscription charge or by periodically purchasing from the dealer. Trading directly with other collectors at conventions or by mail is still another common way of expanding one's collection.

In addition to the ready availability of paperback books their design also encourages acquisition. They take up relatively little space, in contrast to hardcover books or most other collectible materials. Paperbacks are usually numbered on the spine and front cover by imprint and, more recently, by series, and booksellers specializing in used paperbacks often arrange their titles within their stores or in their catalogs by publisher imprint number. Because numbers run sequentially, usually from the earliest publication dates, the collector also has a ready-made arrangement for shelving volumes.

Despite the prices noted on the "Ten Most-Wanted" list, the vast majority of paperback books published in the 1940s and 1950s at twenty-five, thirty-five, and fifty cents will cost the collector little more than two or four times the original cover prices in most secondhand-book outlets. In thrift shops and the like, they generally sell for less, sometimes under their original cover price.

As with all types of collecting, paperbacks of particular kinds or types are more in demand than others. Commonly these books are wanted for their scarcity or for features that make them unusual or attractive. The remainder of this section identifies some of these books or book series and suggests the features that make them desirable to collectors.

Certain paperback imprints and series have achieved particular popularity among collectors. Most often their popularity

THIS PAGE AND FOLLOWING. Obscure imprints of the 1940s (all illustrators unknown):

Handi-Books (1944).

Black Knight (1946).

Bart House (1946).

Hangman's House (1946).

stems from cover designs and illustrations. Among the most sought after are the Ace Double Novels (see Plates 5 and 34a) and the pulp-covered Popular Library and Avon titles (see Plates 9, 17, and 28a–f) of the late 1940s and early 1950s. Bennett Cerf once described postwar volumes with this cover art as "books that had beautiful girls on the jackets but there were no jackets on the beautiful girls."

With the exception of their very first titles, the back covers of early Dell books presented sketches of important settings described in the text. These mapbacks were published from 1943 to 1953. The early airbrush front covers in the mapback series, created by artist Gerald Gregg and others, more than complement the intriguing crime scenes sketched on the back covers. (See Plates 29a–d.)

Obscure and defunct imprints make particularly challenging and satisfying goals for collectors. Usually printed in quantities smaller than those of the major imprints, these books had formats that differed little from the other mass market publications of their time. Their edition totals usually do not exceed more than a hundred or so titles, and sometimes they number less than a half dozen. Lion Library, Black Knight, and Handi-Books are a few of the dozens of colorfully named softcover imprints that appeared briefly in the first twenty years of contemporary mass market publishing.

Paperback imprints, both American and foreign, that preceded the publication of the first Pocket Books editions are also desirable. Dime novels (see page 29), for instance, have a large worldwide society of collectors who have exchanged information and enthusiasm for over half a century. Since 1974 in Great Britain an enthusiastic group of Penguin book collectors has published a newsletter for members throughout the globe. Tauchnitz and Albatross Books also are collected around the world (see page 25).

Early-twentieth-century collectible American imprints include the Little Blue Books of Emanuel Haldeman-Julius; the Boni brothers' imprints, Charles Boni Paper Books and Boni-Books (see page 32); and the Blue, Red, and Gold Seal imprints of Modern Age Books, Inc. But perhaps the most enthusiastically sought-after publications of the pre-Pocket Books era are the $4\frac{7}{16}'' \times 6''$ imprints of Bantam Publications, Inc., of

Los Angeles, California. A series of twenty-nine books published by Western Publishing and Lithographing, they were distributed mainly on the West Coast and sold through vending machines in the late 1930s. They have no direct historical connection with Bantam Books.

Interest in this and other hard-to-obtain paperback imprints has lessened recently. Paperback books, like other collectible items, are subject to fashion, influenced as much by the attention paid to them by collectors' publications and booksellers as by any inherent value or scarcity. Another phenomenon to which paperbacks are subject is *temporary rarity*. Bibliophile John Carter described the situation a half century ago:

> A change of taste or a new discovery stimulates interest among collectors in a book or a category of books hitherto not much regarded; the copies available are snapped up; and until the flow of supply gets under way through the regular channels, a temporary scarcity results, often accompanied by an artificially high price. It is of course notorious that a high price, well advertised, draws books out of their hiding places, whether in the maid's bedroom or the squire's study.

From time to time each major publisher has produced a series, a set of books of similar design and format within an imprint, which today's collectors vie with one another to complete. Among the most collectible are Dell's ten-cent editions (or "Dimers"), as well as their First Edition and Great Mystery Library series (see Plates 30a and b). Others are the sixty-one titles in Pyramid's Green Door series and the fourteen titles of the Gold Medal classic murder trials series. The volumes in this last set, each of which recounts an actual court case, rely on the original trial manuscripts. Each title in this Fawcett series begins with the words "The Girl . . ."

The *Pocket Book of Old Masters* (Pocket Books #578), with sixty-four internal illustrations, was the first mass market book printed by sheet-fed gravure. Published in 1949, it inaugurated a short series of heavily illustrated books dealing with various fine arts subjects. Almost ten years passed before another mass market publisher attempted a similarly designed series.

Most Los Angeles Bantams appeared with typographic covers; a few carried illustrated wrappers. Measuring 4³/₁₆'' x 6'', both were probably published in 1939.

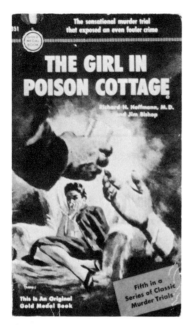

Gold Medal classic murder trial series, all illustrated by the prolific Baryé Phillips. LEFT: 1952. CENTER: 1953. RIGHT: 1953.

Several mass market publishers issued literary magazines in mass market format in the 1950s. These usually contained original works by prominent and up-and-coming writers. The longest-running and most collectible are the twenty-two volumes of *New World Writing,* which was sponsored for seven years by New American Library and then taken over by Lippincott, a trade publisher. Works-in-progress and short stories by writers such as Dylan Thomas, Jack Kerouac, Joseph Heller, and Truman Capote first appeared in this series.

Traditional book collecting stresses the acquisition of the earliest edition of any one of several types, i.e., first editions, first printings, or first American editions of a famous author or title; or the first edition of a publisher, imprint, or series. Some publishers printed sample editions before actually producing a full series of books. In 1929 Charles Boni issued a sample copy of *The Bridge of San Luis Rey* for his paperback book club imprint. (See Plates 31a–c.) Robert de Graff printed Pearl Buck's *The Good Earth* as a sample Pocket Books edition (see pages 36 and 37). Almost a year before publication of its Gold Medal series,

Fawcett issued *The Best from True, the Man's Magazine,* an anthology of articles selected from its mass-circulation periodical.

Publishers sometimes issue special pre-publication review editions of lead paperback titles. Usually given away to retail and wholesale book buyers or to reviewers and other opinion makers, these editions do not display the cover design of the finished edition. To testmarket certain titles, publishers today may distribute the same title with different cover prices and different cover designs to targeted areas of the country.

One of the most common aims of the book collector is to acquire the earliest editions of books by particular authors. Starting in 1950, perhaps as many as 25 percent of all new editions issued in mass market paperback publishing have been original publications. Some publisher imprints, such as Dell's First Editions and Fawcett's Gold Medal series, were almost exclusively originals (see Plates 32a and b).

Among American writers who have had book-length works first appear as mass market paperbacks are Edward Albee, Nelson Algren, Ray Bradbury, James Cain, Erskine Caldwell, Raymond Chandler, John Ciardi, John Dos Passos, Shelby Foote, John Gardner, Langston Hughes, William Inge, Jack Kerouac, Erica Jong, Sinclair Lewis, Mary McCarthy, J. P. Marquand, Horace McCoy, John D. MacDonald, John O'Hara, Ogden Nash, John Steinbeck, Gore Vidal, Kurt Vonnegut, Jr., Cornell Woolrich, Herman Wouk, and Richard Wright. Many writers have also revised and updated books for softcover editions after initial hardcover publication. Vonnegut's *The Sirens of Titan* lays claim to being the first paperback original (Dell First Edition B138, published in 1959) to be reprinted later in hardcover, thus reversing the traditional direction of publication.

Collecting an author's softcover editions from their earliest appearance allows one to compare the "packaging" the writer has received. A book—or an author—may capture new praise and esteem as the years advance, thus enabling or requiring the publisher to redesign the book to attract new or expanded markets. (See Plates 33a–g.)

The first mass market appearance in 1952 of George Orwell's *Burmese Days* (Popular Library #459) carried suggestive cover art and a front-cover blurb promising "a saga of jungle hate and

A precursor of the Fawcett Gold Medal series, published May 1949, measuring 4³⁄₁₆″ x 6¼″.

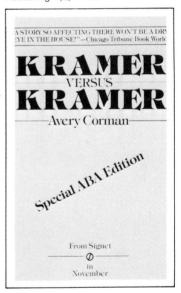

Prepublication Signet issued in 1978.

Collecting

125

lust." Succeeding editions of this work were treated more conservatively as Orwell's *Animal Farm* and *Nineteen Eighty-Four* gained critical and academic recognition in the United States throughout the 1950s and 1960s. Reflecting the mores and times of the society in which the books were published, the various editions in the evolution of a particular title can be a most entertaining and stimulating rationale for softcover collecting. They can lead to endless hours of insight and speculation. (See Plates 13a-h.)

Like well-known authors and their individual titles, the evolution of all of the major fiction genres can be approached through the packaging each has received since the rise of mass market paperbacks. Because paperback publishers were not bashful in copying one another's designs, a successful layout would inspire, as it still does today, overnight imitation.

Especially interesting and valuable for this kind of comparison are those genres that first realized twentieth-century popularity in a paperback rather than a hardcover format. These include the gothic romances of the sixties, the historical romances of the seventies, and sophisticated spy novels, macho fiction, adult Westerns, and fantasy fiction. The paperback explosion of the 1940s and 1950s also opened new markets for pulp fiction categories such as hardboiled detective novels, traditional romances, Westerns, and science fiction.

Although mass market paperbacks have measured roughly either $4\frac{1}{4}'' \times 7\frac{1}{8}''$ or $4\frac{1}{8}'' \times 6\frac{1}{2}''$, a variety of different sizes have been attempted at one time or another by mass market houses, including some bound on the short side, similar to the Armed Forces Editions (see page 47). Softcover books with dust jackets published in the 1940s are also prize collectibles (see Plates 34a–c). The Ace Double Novels (see page 51), published from 1952 to 1965, had two front covers to match the two different novels inside. Other publishers have imitated Ace's double packaging with modest success. The 1940s and 1950s saw some mass market publishers, most notably Dell and Avon, produce digest-size publications (roughly $5\frac{1}{4}'' \times 7\frac{5}{7}''$), which were marketed and distributed more like magazines than books. These frequently contained pulp-style covers more outrageous than their rack-size cousins. (See Plates 35a–d.)

In the late 1940s Doubleday issued Permabooks, a series of paperback-size publications with laminated board covers. Today, collectors label these "hardbacks." The Permabooks series switched to paper covers in 1951. In the early 1960s Avon's book manufacturer, W. F. Hall, rounded off the upper and lower right corners of the publisher's new editions. This dimensional change lasted only a few years, however.

Quality control in the manufacture of paperback books was never an industry strength, and errors in cover printing and binding occur even today. Pocket Books' *The Reward* (#81237), published in 1977, attributes authorship to Max Brand on its cover and copyright page, and incorrectly to Zane Grey on the ad card and title page. Mistakes like these are relatively easy to correct when the book is reissued. However, in 1946, when Pocket Books printed #396, *Laugh with Leacock,* page 4 was blank. The error was caught, but only after some copies of the printing were bound. As a result, a portion of the printing carried between pages 4 and 5 a tipped-in card headlined "Printers do make mistakes!" and giving the text, the remainder of a four-page story that should have concluded on page 4.

In this regard, note this comment of a collector, which appeared in the first issue of *Paperback Quarterly:*

A Perma "hardback" published in 1949.

> At first glance, one might think I own two copies of *Conan the Avenger* by Robert E. Howard, Bjorn Nyberg, and L. Sprague De Camp (Ace Conan Book #10). The truth is I don't own a copy of *Conan the Avenger* at all—or at least not a complete copy. I do have two books with the *Conan the Avenger* cover but once inside, the story changes . . . literally. One copy indeed has the "Avenger" title page and provides an exciting "Avenger" story until page 162, where without warning it becomes the 195th page of *Conan the Conqueror* (Ace Conan Book #9). It remains *Conan the Conqueror* until the end of the book on page 224. *(Conan the Avenger* is supposed to have 192 pages.)
>
> The other copy also has *The Avenger* cover, but the title page is *Conan the Conqueror,* which it remains until page 34. This time with no warning of page number inconsistencies, the 35th page becomes *Conan the Avenger* and re-

mains such until the end of the book on page 192. Apparently the paperback binder really goofed.

Errors in editing, printing, and binding such as these are not only fun to discover but also add value to the book. When these mistakes occur in a work of a well-known author its value is greatly increased, as the printing is sought by book collectors not primarily interested in softcover titles.

From time to time softcover publishers make up special presentation copies of books, usually autographed by well-known authors. These distinctive copies are often given to influential people to please or further enhance the reputation of the author. In 1953 two hundred signed copies of Ray Bradbury's Ballantine edition of *Fahrenheit 451* were bound with asbestos material and given away.

In 1966, when Pope Paul VI visited the United States, one of the rarest of paperback editions was made. Pocket Books and the American Book-Stratford Press made up a fifteen-copy, morocco-leather-bound, slipcased edition of *Pacem in Terris: Proceedings of the International Convention on the Requirements of Peace* held in New York the year before. Pocket Books earlier had issued the report in a mass market edition.

Uniqueness of a different sort centers on those individually numbered titles that Pocket Books issued in the forties. Late in 1940 Pocket Books began to be very impressed with its own sales figures, which started to exceed in number of copies sold those of any other publisher, hardbound or paperback. For about an eight-year period they kept count of their unit sales in much the same way that McDonald's today adds up its hamburger sales.

Dale Carnegie's *How to Win Friends and Influence People* for a time outsold all other Pocket Books titles combined. In 1940 the company arranged with its printer to have each copy individually numbered on the front-cover headband. Immediately after the close of World War II, Pocket resumed this kind of numbering, but this time put serial figures on each of their publications. Impressive strings of nine-digit numbers adorned the headbands as Pocket Books combined all of its past printing figures. Each unit was numbered consecutively, based on the total number of Pocket Books copies printed since 1939. The first title printed with the unique, individual serial numbers was Hervey Allen's

Action at Aquila, Pocket Books #370, published in the spring of 1946. By the end of the year, however, this practice was discontinued.

Until the widespread use of high-speed offset printing equipment in the 1970s, internal illustration, especially half-tones and color plates, was not common to mass market paperbacks. Illustrations that did appear in the texts were usually line cuts reduced from the original hardcover edition. Those that were original in the softcover edition, such as illustrations in pre- and postwar Pocket Books titles, are still joys to the eye.

The most-sought-after titles with internal illustrations are the Bantam endpaper editions, which appeared early in the company's history and were discontinued by the end of 1947. Illustrated by the artists who did the front-cover artwork, these drawings frequently were maps or bird's-eye views of settings described in the text.

COVER ART COLLECTING

Uniting all paperback book collectors, as either a primary or secondary *raison d'être,* is the attraction of the cover art. Laughed and scoffed at or treasured and loved, early paperback covers appeal to people of all ages and backgrounds for their existence and identity, independent of the text they wrap. The laminations and varnishes used on the surfaces of early paperbacks for protection and gloss tend to keep the book in almost as good condition today as when they were first applied. The outside cover of a book acquired by a collector in a preserved state is more likely to continue to resist fading and retain its sparkle than the paper of the text, which is more than likely to yellow and get brittle with age.

Just as collectors of imprints attempt to acquire all of a publisher's output, so do collectors of cover art frequently try to gather all examples of an artist's cover work. Collecting prolific artists who have worked for different publishers and illustrated for many years is a particularly challenging undertaking. Artists like Harry Bennett, George Gross, and Lou Marchetti painted covers beginning in the early 1950s and continue to illustrate today. Their work is generally signed and, provided the signature was not cropped off the picture when the cover was finally designed and printed, relatively easy to identify. (See Plates 36a–c.)

Frequently, however, artists did not sign their works or used different names at various times or on various categories of publications. Many used different artistic styles for different genres. Positive identification is further complicated because the artistic styles of experienced artists evolve through the years, frequently following overall trends in cover illustrations. Successful and innovative illustrators have seen many unsigned imitations of their style appear on softcovers, some so similar that they themselves cannot determine authenticity.

Popular among collectors are paperback cover artists whose work also appears in other media. Several of the better-known illustrators have established reputations among collectors of comics and pulp magazines. Among these are Rudolph Belarski, Earle Bergey, and Norman Saunders. Incidentally, books with covers that originally appeared on magazines or comics command some of the highest catalog prices today.

The Curtis Publishing Company, owner of *The Saturday Evening Post,* was one of the principal partners in the founding of Bantam Books. For nineteen years Curtis also handled the book publisher's sales and distribution to independent wholesalers. Not surprisingly, then, *Post* artists Steve Dohanos, Robert Doares, Hy Rubin, Bernard d'Andrea, and others also created early Bantam covers.

Recently, many illustrators who achieved popularity in paperback form have had collections of their art published or printed on calendars. Most prominent are science fiction and fantasy illustrators Frank Frazetta, Kelly Freas, and Boris Vallejo, as well as Frank McCarthy, James Bama, Robert Abbett, and political cartoonist Bill Mauldin.

As noted earlier, the range of artistic styles in mass market paperback cover art does not stray very far from representational illustration. However, from time to time cover artists, particularly in science fiction works, have shown the influences of abstract impressionism, cubism, expressionism, surrealism, primitivism, and, as one might expect, pop art. Unusual paperback illustrative styles are still another category of collecting.

More common, however, are collectors attracted by illustration categories that parallel the contents of such book genres as Westerns, mysteries, romances, and fantasy and science fiction. Clichés in these illustrations are endemic, and exceptions to the clichés intriguing. Traditionally, Western covers called for guns and horses, mysteries required a murder weapon, and science fiction a spaceship. Throughout these genres certain themes in the realistic cover-art styles demand more attention from collectors than others. Far outshadowing all other motifs are the "good girl" and bondage covers that became prominent shortly after World War II. Sex, overt and subtle, straight and kinky, has probably inspired more people to assemble paperback collections than any other single feature. The same features that attracted drugstore buyers in the 1940s compel purchase by collectors in the eighties—affirmations of the permanence of the illustration and its effectiveness as commercial art.

More reflective of the time and the mood of the country than the overtly sexual expressions are the backwoods themes portrayed by James Avati for Erskine Caldwell's books (see Plates 16c and d) and the illustrations for the urban street literature of James Farrell, Irving Shulman, and Benjamin Appel. Direct visual offshoots of this fiction category were the covers of the World War II novels that appeared in the late 1940s and early 1950s. Prominent on the covers of Signets and Bantams were hard-nosed but kind GIs in the company of homeless waifs or prostitutes.

Specific characters, especially detectives, appear and reappear in softcover art. Especially collectible are those not modeled after movie or television actors; the most interesting are Nero Wolfe, Philo Vance, and Hercule Poirot. Reaching back into the nineteenth century, however, detective Nick Carter and his four separate mass market incarnations also demand special attention.

The practice of paperback publishers of reissuing the same title with a new cover is fairly common. In the 1940s, however, several major paperback companies printed fresh dust jackets to envelop an earlier edition, and only a few dozen have been recorded. Perhaps even more interesting are publisher economy measures where the same cover art adorns two completely different titles.

Another challenge is collecting by type of object illustrated. Because of their often photographic details, the vintage paperbacks of the late 1940s and 1950s abound with objects such as hats, dresses, and automobiles that accurately record the society in which the artist, as well as the characters in the book, lived. The world of postwar America can be pieced together from the street scenery, bedroom decor, and architecture of the softcover stage settings of the 1940s and 1950s. (See Plates 37a–d, 38a–d, and 39a–d.)

(See Plates 37a–d, 38a–d, and 39a–d.)

OTHER COLLECTIBLE FEATURES

Publisher logos can be as much an inspiration to collectors as the titles and cover art they adorn. Like the evolution of author and title cover art, their mutations are interesting to collect and speculate on.

The Bantam rooster, an inspiration of now-independent publisher Bernard Geis and first shown by Robert Foster, was fattened up in the 1950s when the original symbol was accused of being emaciated. A medical diagnosis was also made of a revision to the original Penguin logo. The intent of the change was to "portray a light-hearted dancing version of the familiar bird; to the more discriminating eye it always seemed to be a Penguin in the throes of appendicitis."

Perhaps no paperback logo has generated more recognition and affection than the appealing evolutions experienced by the Pocket Books wallaby. Christened "Gertrude" after the mother-in-law of her first designer, Frank J. Lieberman, she has undergone at least a half dozen major and minor mutations, including one drawn by Walt Disney.

Finally, nonillustrative elements also can inspire acquisition, such as titles (my favorite: Rona Barrett's recent Bantam Original, *How You Can Look Rich and Achieve Sexual Ecstasy*) and title changes (my favorite: Ludwig Lewisohn's American Penguin #649, *The Tyranny of Sex,* from the original *The Case of Mr. Crump).* Promotional blurbs, particularly those on the headbands of the pulpy Avon and Popular Library covers, may invite gentle derision or sarcasm. However, the meter and alliteration of the plot summary heading *All Dames Are Dynamite* (Novel Library #29) is impossible to resist, "A street girl gives her real heart to a guy in the gutters of Hell."

The deeper people get into collecting paperback books, the more likely they will be caught up by the ephemeral objects connected with the industry: old catalogs, posters, advertising, flyers, and perhaps even the early wood and metal racks with the publisher's name and logo prominently displayed. Publishers have occasionally given out premiums with their books. In 1978, with Gimone Hall's *Rapture's Mistress,* New American Library gave out packets of bath oil of the same name. However, eighteen years earlier Monarch Books had already topped this ploy. In the spring of 1960 the publisher announced that selected titles should be perfumed. They promised the smell would last several months—the first would be Chanel No. 5. In the future, Westerns are planned with a leather scent, while cookbooks might smell of freshly baked bread!

Author- and illustrator-autographed copies are yet another kind of collecting, more specialized than any other kind. The autographed-book collector may be rewarded with unique discoveries that are not only a treasure to own but are part of the lore of paperback history. On November 21, 1941, Dale Carnegie autographed for his publisher, Robert de Graff, a copy of the eleventh printing of Pocket Books #68, *How to Win Friends and Influence People:*

A 1941 Industries Cooperation poster.

My Dear Bob:

You certainly know how to win friends. At least you won me years ago.

And anybody who sells a million copies of a book I wrote certainly knows how to influence people. Yes, Bob, here is one book you published that you don't need to read.

You ought to draw a deep, abiding satisfaction from the splendid work you are doing. This world needs more Bob de Graffs.

/s/ Dale Carnegie

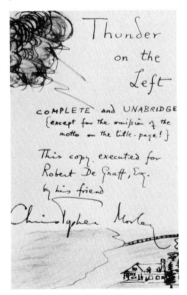

Author Christopher Morley drew this one-of-a-kind cover for the 1940 edition of *Thunder on the Left,* and presented it, pasted over the printed cover, to Robert de Graff.

Collectors with good-sized bankrolls may try to acquire original manuscripts or printer's galleys or page proofs. With the recent growth of interest in vintage paperback illustration, some original artwork of old paperbacks has become available for purchase through dealers who specialize in commercial art. The quality of the art, the reputation of the artist, and the condition of the painting all influence the cost of original paperback art. Prices may range from $100 to several thousands of dollars.

Collecting

133

In spite of, or perhaps because of, all these collecting paths, one should not forget the inspiration that leads many first to pick up and purchase a secondhand title: the desire to read it. To purchase an old paperback with the intent to read its message as well as add it to one's collection is the noblest of all reasons for collecting.

One note of caution must be stressed: Many vintage paperbacks, particularly those manufactured during and ten years or so after World War II, are printed on paper with high ground-wood content and are bound with animal glue. The pages of these titles usually are yellowed and brittle, and often separate from their spines. One sign of this condition is a loud crack at opening. This is usually followed by the discovery that the volume has come apart in your hands. Often the only permanent feature is the laminated or varnished cover. Because it is so easy physically to damage older paperback titles, reducing both satisfaction and book value, collectors seek out duplicate copies to read, and they often try to upgrade their collections by locating editions in better states of condition than copies currently owned. The replaced copies are usually sold or traded.

Paperback books should be protected from extreme temperatures, moisture, the sun, and excessive artificial light. Book preservationists recommend a temperature of 68 degrees F or less and a relative humidity of 50 percent. Above 70 percent humidity, the growth of damaging mold is likely to occur; below 40 percent, the pages can dry out and yellow.

Many collectors keep their books in plastic sleeves for preservation. This wrapping not only keeps moisture and dust off the books but also protects cover laminations and finishes. Darker covers—purples and blacks—as well as metallic covers are particularly prone to marring when rubbed. Only plastic sleeves made of stable chemicals, such as Dupont's Mylar brand, are recommended. Plastic that is not chemically inert can react with the materials of the book and defeat preservation. Protective sleeves may be purchased through library supply houses or through dealers who advertise in the collector publications listed in the "Further Reading" section of this book.

To their dismay, collectors often find that the most interesting titles to collect and read are in the poorest shape because of the number of times they were read and then passed along to others.

One is hard pressed, for example, to find mint copies of early Mickey Spillane editions, the required reading of the high school corridors, college dorms, and army barracks of the 1950s.

In a tongue-in-cheek look at paperback history in 1968, John Leonard, the *New York Times Book Review* editor at the time, identified another reason for the scarcity of some paperbacks by extolling these "virtues":

> . . . they can be stuffed in purses, left on buses, dropped in toilets, used as coasters, eaten and thrown away. Their covers can be ripped off! *Their spines can be broken!*
>
> To buy a paperback today is to buy the means of revenging oneself on Western culture.

As with fine art, the condition of a vintage paperback book is a prime factor in its value. Some collectors will buy only editions in near-perfect condition. The binding must be secure and tight, pages unyellowed, the cover uncracked and unmarked, the lamination (if there is any) unseparated, the colors of the cover and the edge stain unfaded. Buying sight unseen from a dealer's catalog, of course, does not allow the collector to examine the title before purchase. However, reputable dealers will return your money if, soon after its arrival through the mail, you are not satisfied with the condition of the book.

Most dealer catalogs are arranged either alphabetically by author or by publisher imprint and number. In either case, in addition to sale price, the most informative catalogs give author, full title, publisher and publisher number, printing, and printing date. In the most comprehensive catalogs, features of bibliographic and historical interest are noted, such as the original title if it was changed by the reprinter. Unusual design and illustration features are described and the cover artist noted if identifiable.

The condition of the book is usually indicated on a scale that includes at least four states: poor, good, fine, and mint. There is, however, no universally accepted grading scale among paperback collectors and dealers. *The Paperback Price Guide* (see "Further Reading") offers an eight-point scale that may be too fine for many dealers. Incidentally, most used-book dealers will not handle a paperback that is not at the upper end of the grading scale.

Exceptions are very hard-to-find editions. Blemishes such as cover markings, damage, and missing pages are cited in reputable price lists.

It is obvious that booksellers who comply with the above procedures must spend many laborious hours preparing their price lists, checking for accuracy, and trying to grade their offerings honestly. These sales lists are evidence of the history and growth of paperback book collecting; as tools of reference and research for now and the future they also are worthy of preservation. For many dealers, preparing sales catalogs is as much a labor of love as it is a profitable enterprise. To those who perform this task must go the sincere appreciation of collectors.

FUTURE COLLECTIBLE PAPERBACKS

As the availability of vintage publications declines, the boundaries of what titles are collectible will expand. Imprints of the pre-1959 era that were once passed over will become more desirable for collectors and dealers. Any series, such as the silver- and gold-spined Pocket Books and Pocket Cardinals, where the illustrator is noted on the edition, will be increasingly sought. The "photo-novels" of movie tie-ins produced in the 1970s are also a good bet for collectors, as are any of the newer series of paperback fiction where the story line is carried by cartoon-like illustrations or photographs, books similar to the *fumetti* literature of Italy, Spain, and Latin America. Foreign paperback imprints, such as those published after World War II in Great Britain, Spain, and Latin America, that imitate American designs will also be favored. Especially collectible will be those editions that are translations of popular American paperbacks.

The early editions of writers who later achieved notoriety naturally will find an eager collector audience. Among the more recent and better-known examples are John Jakes and Howard Hunt (see Plate 32). Paper editions that Jakes and Hunt wrote in the 1950s and 1960s have gained added value from the fame their authors achieved in the 1970s.

Since the late 1970s the *West Coast Review of Books* has cited the best original paperbacks of the year. These "Porgie" awards include citations in the categories of fantasy novel, historical romance, adventure novel, and contemporary fiction. If not now, then at some future date these prizewinners will be collected in earnest.

Sponsored by the Association of American Publishers, in 1980 the first American Book Awards cited outstanding covers of both trade and mass market houses. In the late 1970s *Marketing Bestsellers,* a trade magazine for paperback and magazine retailers and wholesalers, began citing the best cover art for each month. In 1980 the magazine announced its first annual awards at a party where each winning publisher received a plaque. Chances are these cited covers will one day be eagerly sought.

Just as the obscure and short-lived imprints of the 1940s and 1950s are collectible, more recent paperback casualties, such as Baronet, Dale, and Condor, which existed for only a short time in the late seventies, will no doubt one day be in demand.

Specific series that have a new twist or angle also seem to be a good investment gamble. The covers of the Foul Play Press, a trade paperback series begun in 1979, feature photographs of authors or booksellers associated with mystery fiction posing as victims of murder. One of the first volumes in the series presents the stabbed "corpse" of Edward Gorey. Zebra Books' mass market series, Mystery Puzzlers, gives clues for solving whodunits in internal illustrations as well as on the front cover. The final chapter is sealed so that the solution to the crime is not readily available. On the final page of the chapter the pictorial clues are explained.

The multiple and gimmick covers that exploded on bookstore shelves in the 1970s will undoubtedly fascinate collectors of the eighties and beyond. Collectors are challenged by the task of finding copies of all six covers—white, yellow, blue, pink, green, and tangerine—wrapping Bantam's first printing of Alvin Toffler's *Future Shock.* Issued in 1971, it was the first of what has become the frequent practice of publishers to use multiple covers, usually using different illustrations on the first printings of blockbuster titles. The fold-out, die-cut, step-back, foil-stamped, and foil-embossed covers used on lead and blockbuster titles will also attract attention from softcover collectors in the future.

In a conversation with the author, Robert de Graff once summarized his guiding rule of thumb when he selected cover designs for his books: "The cover should be a window through which you can see into the book." This same guideline, only slightly amended, is appropriate for paperback collectors. Whether one is prompted by nostalgia, curiosity, or investment considerations to acquire softcover titles, the cover design is the most dependable gauge for determining value—a window (or keyhole perhaps) through which one can measure the collectibility of a paperback book.

Further Reading

Though long out of print, *The Paperbound Book in America* by Frank L. Schick (Bowker, 1958) has no rival as a record of the history of paperback publishing in the United States to 1956. Thoroughly researched, it is based in large part on personal interviews with the founders of mass market publishing houses.

Paperbacks, U.S.A.: A Graphic History by Piet Schreuders (Blue Dolphin Enterprises, 1981) contains a wealth of information on the history of vintage paperbacks and the people who designed and made them.

Geoffrey O'Brien's lyrical celebration of American paperback detective fiction of the 1940s and 1950s, *Hardboiled America* (Van Nostrand Reinhold, 1981) is the most entertaining book yet written about softcover publishing.

Although it really only covers the success of one particular publishing company, *The Bantam Story* by Clarence Petersen (Bantam Books, 2nd ed., 1975) outlines the major events that have occurred in contemporary mass market publishing and looks behind the scenes at how most softcover publishers operate. It may be obtained free of charge by writing to Bantam Books, 666 Fifth Avenue, New York, NY 10019.

Roger H. Smith's *Paperback Parnassus* (Bowker, 1976) is an in-depth study of paperback distribution, both trade and mass market. It is based on a 1975 series of articles in *Publishers Weekly.*

COLLECTING *Paperback Primer: A Guide for Collectors* by Thomas L. Bonn (Pecan Valley Press, 1982) was designed as a detailed introduction to vintage paperback collecting. It includes an extensive, annotated bibliography of paperback book history and may be obtained by sending $3.50 to Paperback Quarterly, 1710 Vincent Street, Brownwood, TX 76801.

The single most useful reference book for collectors is Robert Reginald's *Cumulative Paperback Index, 1939-59* by Robert Reginald and M. R. Burgess (Gale Research, 1973). A labor of love, it is an invaluable aid in identifying vintage editions, authors, and titles.

Roundly criticized at publication for inflated price listings, *The Paperback Price Guide* by Kevin Hancer (Harmony Books, 1980) is nonetheless a handy gauge to relative paperback values. A new edition is scheduled for publication in 1982.

Two periodicals are published for students of American paperback publishing and both are enthusiastically recommended: *Paperback Quarterly: Journal of Mass Market Paperback History,* 1710 Vincent Street, Brownwood, TX 76801; and *Collecting Paperbacks ?,* 934 SE 15th Avenue, Portland, OR 97214.

For collectors of Penguin Books, there is the *Penguin Collectors' Society Newsletter,* 5 Primrose Way, Linton, Cambridge, CB1, 6 UD, England.

Additional information on paperback collecting can be found in several contributions in *Collectible Books: Some New Paths,* Jean Peters, ed. (Bowker, 1979).

The Blockbuster Complex by Thomas Whiteside (Wesleyan University Press, 1981), based on the author's widely discussed series of articles in *The New Yorker,* provides an excellent introduction to trends in contemporary American publishing.

Index